Moving

A Comedy

Stanley Price

Samuel French—London
New York – Sydney – Toronto – Hollywood

MOVING

First presented by Toby Rowland for Stoll Productions Ltd at the Queen's Theatre, on 21st January 1981, with the following cast of characters:

Joan Belling	Pamela Blackwood
Peter Belling	Billy Murray
Frank Gladwin	Peter Jeffrey
Sarah Gladwin	Penelope Keith
John Fearnley	Richard Thorp
Beryl Fearnley	Margo Jenkins
Liz Ford	Barbara Ferris
Jimmy Ryan	Roger Lloyd Pack
Jane Gladwin	Miranda Richardson
Len	David Redgrave
Bill	Kevin White
The voice of Ben Gladwin	Clive Merrison

Directed by Robert Chetwyn
Designed by Alan Tagg

The action takes place in the Gladwins' living-room over the course of last summer

Time—the present

A licence issued by Samuel French Ltd to perform this play does not include permission to use the Incidental music specified in this copy. Where the place of performance is already licensed by the Performing Right Society a return of the music used must be made to them. If the place of performance is not so licensed then application should be made to the Performing Right Society, 29 Berners Street, London W1.

A separate and additional Licence from Phonographic Performances Ltd, Ganton House, Ganton Street, London W1 is needed whenever commercial recordings are used.

ACT I

The Gladwins' living-room

It is a spacious, bright room, its proportions those of a late Victorian house of the kind to be found north of the Thames in Hampstead or Highgate, or south of the Thames in Greenwich or Blackheath, occupying practically the whole ground-floor width of the house. There are three basic living areas. Central is a sitting-room comprising a sofa, two armchairs and a coffee-table. Downstage right is the desk and chair where Sarah Gladwin works and underneath the window upstage of this are bookshelves stocked with typed manuscripts, box-files and books. The manuscripts spill on to the desk where there is also a phone. On the upstage right wall are further bookshelves and two sets of cupboards. There is a hi-fi system on top of the lower cupboards with a rack of records in one of the cupboards below. Next to the hi-fi system is a tray of drinks with glasses. Upstage left is a small dining-area with a table of the folding variety which could seat eight at a pinch. Upstage of the table is an arched entrance to the kitchen with louver doors that are fixed open. Left is a fireplace which does not look as though it is used much. The decor and furnishings of the room reflect feminine rather than masculine taste, but practical rather than fussy female. The furnishings are comfortable but well-worn, in particular the sofa and armchairs, everything being at least six years old so there is no hint of trendiness. Clearly everything has been bought to last and some pieces have lasted better than others. The walls and ceiling could do with a lick of paint and there are a few mildly ominous cracks, especially in the corners over the door. The room is currently in a state of impeccable neatness. The books are all on their shelves, the maga- zines carefully laid out on the coffee-table, the manuscripts piled as evenly as possible on the desk, the cushions on the chairs and sofa all plumped up

When the CURTAIN *rises the stage is in total darkness and the following pre-recorded voices are heard. They are loud and distinct now as they should be throughout*

Sarah's voice . . . and this is the kitchen. All the cupboards are fitted so we'll be leaving them behind . . . and this is the main bedroom . . .

Woman's voice It's a nice size.

Sarah's voice And this is our bathroom. I hate that word the agents use— *en suite*. We put the shower in four years ago—and that too.

Woman's voice Yes, a lot of bathrooms seem to have *them* these days.

Frank's voice . . . it's gas-fired.

Sarah's voice . . . I think the agents call it "pine-clad".

Frank's voice . . . carpet's negotiable.

The doorbell rings and the Lights come up

Sarah's voice . . . as a junk-room.
Frank's voice . . . yes, we knocked through.
Sarah's voice . . . yes, *en suite.*

Sarah Gladwin opens the living-room door and shows in Peter and Joan Belling. Sarah is in her early forties. She is casually, but neatly dressed. Her manner, at least in front of potential buyers, is firm and energetic. Peter Belling is about thirty-five, very carefully dressed in the most expensive casual clothes. There is a sharp, sleek, totally contemporary look to him. His wife, Joan, is a year or two younger, and mirrors, in a female way, her husband's off-work Sunday look. What she wears is equally expensive, but whereas her husband looks totally trendy, on her it all looks mildly tarty

Sarah Come in. I'm afraid we've still got some people here.
Peter We were told seven-thirty was convenient.
Sarah Yes. You're not early. The others are late. I'm sure they won't be long. Please make yourselves comfortable.

Sarah goes out, shutting the door

Alone in the room, Peter and Joan snoop around, blatantly inquisitive, as only prospective buyers can be

Joan Full house. Maybe we should have come this morning.
Peter If the agent puts an ad. in the Sundays with their home number, everybody turns up. It means they're desperate. (*He tries the light-switch by the door. Nothing happens as there is no centre light*) That doesn't work. (*He wanders over to the bookshelves and glances at the books*) They've got a lot of medical books. He must be a doctor.

Joan opens the lower cupboard

Joan (*looking over the gramophone records*) Lots of records too. Mostly classical. No. There's some decent stuff here. Probably belongs to their kids. (*She goes and glances off into kitchen*)

Peter goes to look out of the window, and gets out a compass

Peter House faces east. Probably dark this side in the afternoon.
Joan It says it's got five bedrooms.
Peter And there's no garage. And no off-street parking. (*He looks at what's on the desk*)
Joan (*going into the kitchen*) I like the kitchen off. Don't have to miss all the conversation when you're cooking. (*She comes out of the kitchen*)
Peter I've seen their ad. before. It's been on the market for months. And they've just dropped the price seven thousand.
Joan Could do with some paint.
Peter Plenty of cracks.
Joan All old houses have those. It looks fairly solid. It's a nice size room.
Peter (*opening the upper drinks cupboard*) They must like liqueurs. There's bottles of them in here.

Frank Gladwin comes in. He is a fit-looking man in his mid-to-late forties. He wears corduroy trousers, an open-necked plain shirt, and battered suede shoes. He has a slightly distracted look, and is clearly surprised to see the Bellings there, and looking in his drinks cupboard

Peter quickly shuts the cupboard door

Frank Oh. You're the—
Joan The Bellings. Your wife let us in.
Frank Ah!
Peter Told us to wait in here.
Frank Bit of a log-jam. She's just finishing with another couple.
Peter Busy day, eh!
Frank Exhausting. I imagine you've had a good look round in here while you were waiting.
Joan Yes. It's a nice room.
Frank Anything I can tell you before I show you the rest of the house?
Joan Doesn't say what sort of heating.
Frank Gas-fired.
Joan There's a rose, but no centre light.
Frank No. We—er—prefer lamps.
Peter But they don't switch on from the door? (*He indicates the main light-switch at the door*)
Frank Afraid not. We planned to do it if we redecorated.
Peter When do you hope to move?
Frank As soon as we've sold this.
Peter Have you found somewhere else?
Frank Yes. More or less.
Peter Bit of a tough time to sell a house, isn't it?

Frank is not at home with the subtleties of business manoeuvres. He clearly resents Peter's manner—the self-conscious shrewdness of a man who thinks he knows how to handle people

Frank Then you've got the same problem.
Joan No. We've got a flat on a lease that's nearly up.
Peter So we've nothing to sell. Are you a doctor?
Frank Why? Aren't you feeling well?
Peter No. I was just looking at some of those medical books, that's all.
Frank I'm a periodontist.
Peter Ah.
Joan Something to do with backs?
Frank No. Gums.
Joan Sorry?
Frank Gums. The things your teeth are in. I try to preserve them. So your teeth don't fall out. I'll show you the rest of the house.

The door opens and Sarah comes in with John and Beryl Fearnley. John is about fifty, a rotund man in a tweed jacket and grey trousers, who exudes solidity. His wife, Beryl, looks several years younger than he. Her clothes, with a mild ethnic influence, looks as though they have been

*hastily pulled out of a drawer. Her fluttery manner is exacerbated by the
tension of the situation. Sarah is surprised to see Frank and the Bellings
still in the living-room*

Sarah Oh hello. We've nearly finished our tour. Mr Fearnley just wants
to measure to see if his piano will fit.

*There is a brief moment while the two respective couples size each other up
as potential rivals. Frank and Sarah are trapped between them, like super-
numeraries in their own house. Sarah tries to act like the gallant hostess at a
sinking cocktail party*

This is Mr and Mrs Fearnley. Mr and Mrs—
Frank Bending.
Sarah Bending.
Peter Belling.
Sarah Belling.
Frank Belling. Sorry. Right, lead on, I'll show you the rest of the house.

He leads the Bellings out past Sarah and the Fearnleys

John (*getting out a retractable steel tape-measure*) I think the window
would be the best place.
Sarah Please do.

John starts measuring the downstage right corner of the room

Beryl It's so hard to find a living-room big enough for a grand piano.
Sarah Do you both play?
Beryl No. Just my husband. I used to play the oboe. I stopped after my
second. My second child, that is. We've got four.
John It would fit nicely here. What's over this room?
Sarah The main bedroom. You'd only keep your wife awake.
John She can sleep through everything except late Beethoven.
Beryl John means late in his career. Beethoven's, I mean. Not late at
night.
Sarah Quite.
John Have you lived here long?
Sarah Fourteen years. But our son's in America, and our daughter's at
college, so the place is just too big for us—now we're on our own.
Beryl It must be strange—a bit lonely—when your children leave home.
Sarah Oh, it is.
John Have you found another house?
Sarah A flat actually—with a nice garden.
John So you want to move as soon as possible?
Sarah We'd like to. Of course, we haven't exchanged contracts on the
flat yet. How old are your children?
Beryl Seventeen, fourteen, twelve and nine. Boy, girl, boy, girl.
John We've rather over-produced for the space we've got.
Beryl We've been looking for ages for something bigger in this district.
Sarah Where are you living now?
John Cranfield Gardens.

Sarah We're practically neighbours.

Beryl We don't want to move out of the district. Our children are so happy in their schools and this would be ideal.

John (*restraining her*) The heating is gas, isn't it?

Sarah Yes. Would you like a drink?

Baryl Oh yes. Thank you.

Sarah Do sit down.

Beryl sits on the sofa, John on the armchair

There's sherry or Scotch. If you've had dinner we've some liqueurs, all rather sticky.

Beryl Sherry for me, please.

Sarah Patients give them to my husband as presents.

John Scotch, please. Just a small one.

Sarah gets the drinks, a sherry for Beryl and Scotch for John

Your husband's a doctor?

Sarah A dentist. A periodontist, actually.

Beryl Oh, that's interesting. Does he practise round here?

Sarah No. He's at a teaching hospital. He does some clinical work there. Soda?

John Yes, please.

Sarah hands them their drinks

Thank you. Cheers. Which way does this room face?

Sarah I should know that, shouldn't I? I think it's north-east. My husband always says that women have no sense of direction.

Beryl John always says that too. I'm terrible when I'm driving. Can't tell left from right, either. I read once that Freud said it was because—

John (*cutting her short again*) Sun in here in the morning, then?

Sarah Yes, it's very light. I tend to work at my desk then.

John What work do you do?

Sarah I read—for a publisher.

Beryl Oh, how interesting. And you can do it at home.

Sarah Yes.

John What do you read?

Sarah Novels mostly.

John You decide whether they're worth publishing or not?

Sarah I give a report. A few other people have a say too.

Frank comes back into the living-room with the Bellings. He looks with dismay at the Fearnleys drinking

Frank Ah, still here. Mrs Bending—

Peter Belling.

Frank —wants to look at the kitchen.

Sarah Of course. Through here.

Again there is a moment where the Bellings and the Fearnleys eye each other as rivals. The Bellings register suspiciously that the Fearnleys have drinks

Sarah switches on the kitchen light and takes the Bellings into the kitchen. Frank stands awkwardly for a moment, waiting for the Fearnleys to leave

John Your wife was saying this room faces north-east.

Frank South-east actually.

John So the sun is in here in the morning.

Frank After eleven in the mornings.

John Can't rely on that in this country, can you?

Sarah We'll be taking the dishwasher and the fridge with us. We'll leave everything else.

Joan And there's a waste-disposal?

Sarah Yes. It works like this.

Sarah switches on the waste-disposal unit and there is a horrible grinding noise. She switches it off at once

Oh, God, there must be a teaspoon down there.

Beryl You must be sorry to be leaving such a nice house?

Frank Yes. But it's too big for us now.

John Your children have left home?

Frank Yes.

Beryl Where's your daughter at college?

Frank Bristol.

Joan What about smells?

Sarah Smells?

Joan Into the living-room when you're cooking.

Sarah I use this fan. It's very effective. (*She switches the fan on but nothing happens so she starts to hit the offending object*)

John indicates he wants a sheet from the notepad

John May I make a few notes?

Frank Yes, please do.

Peter (*coming out of the kitchen*) Your fan's broken I think. There's no garage, is there?

Joan comes out of the kitchen

Frank Afraid not. I usually manage to find a space outside.

Sarah switches off the light and comes out of the kitchen

Peter Yes, but we've got two cars.

Frank My wife's got a Mini. There's usually room for both.

Peter Ours are pretty big. A Lancia and a BMW.

Frank Buy British, eh?

Peter Do you get much traffic on this street?

Sarah A bit in the rush-hour, that's all. People tend to use it as a short cut.

John That happens to all side-streets these days.

There is another awkward silence. Frank looks helplessly at Sarah. The Bellings and the Fearnleys seem determined to outstay each other

Sarah Would *you* like a drink?

Peter No. We've still got another house to look at. We'll talk about it. If we're interested we'll be in touch.

Frank Yes. Call the Estate Agent—Mr Goodis.

Frank escorts the Bellings out to the front door

Sarah turns back to the Fearnleys, whom she clearly prefers as potential buyers

Sarah I hope you haven't got two big cars.

John No. Just one between the six of us.

Beryl I use a bicycle locally.

Frank comes back into the room. He looks determined to dislodge the Fearnleys

Frank Is there anything else I can . . .

John No thanks. We ought to be going.

Beryl It's a lovely house. So spacious. We'd—

John (*cutting her off again*) Like to think about it very seriously.

Frank Have you sold your house yet?

John No, but we've got friends who are very interested.

Beryl We've known them for a long time. They have to move back to London, and they're very keen . . .

John As soon as we've found what we want. Thanks for the drink.

He goes with Frank to the door and goes out

Beryl (*hanging back*) Thank you so much for showing us round.

Sarah You're very welcome. By the way, what did Freud say about women not having a sense of direction?

Beryl (*embarrassed*) He said that—well, it was because women don't have —er—penises.

Sarah Oh.

Beryl Goodbye. Thanks so much.

Beryl goes out

Sarah visibly wilts. She crosses to her desk and picks up a piece of paper that has a list of the day's viewers on it. She goes over and collapses in an armchair and kicks off her shoes

Frank comes back into the room

Frank Is that it for the day?

Sarah Yes.

Frank Thank God. I can mess the place up a bit then. (*He spreads the magazines on the coffee-table*) It feels as if we're living in a shop window.

Sarah I told you. I'm keeping this place tidy till we've sold it. (*She tidies the magazines again*)

He crosses to the drinks tray and helps himself to a Scotch

Frank Do you want something?

Sarah A blood transfusion. I thought they'd never go.

Frank You didn't help. Did you have to offer them a drink? (*He pours a Scotch and soda for Sarah*)

Sarah I think the Fearnleys are interested. And they are almost neighbours.

Frank You offered the others too.

Sarah I knew they wouldn't go till we did.

Frank They didn't even want a drink.

Sarah No, but they wanted to be offered one. Couldn't let the others steal a march on them. That's the sort of people they were.

Frank hands her a Scotch and soda. She drinks some, and tries to perk herself up

The Fearnleys are definitely interested.

Frank Huh! They haven't even put their house on the market yet.

Sarah He said they had friends . . .

Frank How many times have we heard that? These days you're a pariah on the market if you've got a house to sell. Remember the Davidsons— and the Cullens. We gave them drinks too. They practically lived here —and they still couldn't sell their wretched houses—and buy ours.

He takes a big swig of his drink. Sarah sips hers

Sarah I could tell she wanted this house.

Frank He was being cautious.

Sarah But his piano fits. Maybe she'll persuade him to get a bridging-loan.

Frank At twenty per cent? He didn't look like a lunatic to me. Did you find out what he did?

Sarah Civil Servant. Department of Education.

Frank Does his wife work?

Sarah I don't think so. Four kids and a bicycle.

Frank Then he can't afford a bridging-loan. (*He crosses to the drinks and starts to pour himself another Scotch*)

Sarah Do you really need another?

Frank Yes.

There is a gloomy silence

Sarah Those Belling people were obnoxious.

Frank (*sitting on the sofa*) Very keen to tell me they were cash-buyers.

Sarah Lease on their flat up, I suppose?

Frank Yes. Anyway all he wanted was a double-garage. He said he's in the recording industry.

Sarah She looked as if she was a tart.

Frank Then at least they're both working.

Sarah Bringing the price down obviously worked. Everybody came.

Frank I liked it better when nobody came. Anyone else show any interest? (*He drinks*)

Sarah (*consulting her list*) Maybe the Grahams. Except they keep commenting on the cracks in the bedrooms. Maybe we should have had it redecorated.

Frank Waste thousands and have someone come in and re-do it their way.

Sarah What about that Iranian couple?

Frank Oh yes, them. Don't know. She didn't speak English.

Sarah What about him?

Frank He said "very good" all the time.

Sarah Is that all?

Frank No. He said all his money was in Switzerland, and he kept asking how far we were from the airport.

Sarah sips her drink

Sarah The Fearnleys are the best bet.

Frank And if they make an offer it'll be another three or four months buggering around . . .

Sarah Drink depresses you.

Frank It's not drink. It's this past four months. The world and its bloody aunt's been through here. Nobody's buying any more. Everyone's staying put—unless they're emigrating. You know what I think?

Sarah Yes.

Frank I think nobody can afford to eat out anymore, or go to the cinema, or entertain their friends, so when they're fed up watching telly they go out and look at the houses that are up for sale. Sometimes they're even given a free drink. We're too late.

Sarah Whose fault is that? I wanted to move even before Jane went to college. The market was all right then. *You* wouldn't even talk about it.

Frank Let's not go over all that again. Is there any supper?

Sarah Yes. There's some tuna-fish salad in the fridge.

Frank Christ, when did we last have a hot meal?

Sarah gets up

Sarah (*angrily*) In the good old days.

She goes towards the kitchen. Frank gets up, stops her and puts an arm round her

Frank I'm sorry. Sorry. We're both exhausted. It's all been too much.

She nods, near to tears. He looks at his watch

Why don't we go out and eat?

Sarah I thought no-one could afford that any more.

Frank We might manage a curry without a bridging-loan.

Sarah O.K. Where shall we go? The red flock wallpaper? Or the gold flock? I'll go and get ready.

The phone rings and they both look at it apprehensively. Sarah clearly never likes answering the phone, and rarely does. She goes to the door, and hesitates, while he goes to the phone

Maybe it's an offer.

Frank (*answering the phone*) Hello. (*To Sarah*) No, it's not an offer.

She goes out. He waits cautiously till she is out of earshot

(*On the phone*) Yes. Fine. How are you? Yes, I know . . . Yes. I'm sorry about all the delays . . . We do have some people who've made an offer. They're on the point of selling their house . . . Of course, I've only got their word for it . . . Look, Mr Martin, I know you want to exchange contracts on your flat, and I'm sorry if . . . Wouldn't it be better if your solicitor spoke to my solicitor? . . . (*He takes a swig of his drink*) Friday! *This* Friday? That's impossible . . . Of course we haven't changed our minds . . . Yes. I'll phone you. Good-night. (*He slams the phone down, cursing under his breath. He swallows the last of his Scotch*)

Sarah comes in. She has tidied herself up, and wears a short jacket

Sarah (*drawing the curtains* R) Who was it?
Frank Oh, just Bennett, the lab technician. He was having trouble with some splints.
Sarah On Sunday night?
Frank I'm doing surgery tomorrow. Did you decide where?
Sarah Yes. Red flock, and we won't talk about the house. (*She turns out the standard lamp and wall-bracket lights*)
Frank Christ, what else is there?
Sarah I'll tell you about Mrs Fearnley and her penises.

She goes out

Frank *What?*

Frank turns out the light and follows her out, closing the door behind him

Black-out. There are a few moments' silence and then Sarah's and Frank's voices are heard on tape in the darkness

Sarah's voice . . . that used to be my son's bedroom. He's in America. This is our bedroom. With the kitchen *en suite* . . .
Frank's voice (*softly*) Sarah, you're talking in your sleep.

There are grunting, sleepy noises from Sarah. Then the sound of someone getting out of bed, feet hitting the floor, a cupboard door opening and closing quietly

Sarah's voice (*sleepy*) Where are you going?
Frank's voice Can't sleep. Going downstairs for a bit.
Sarah's voice What time is it?
Frank's voice Go back to sleep.

There is the sound of a door opening and closing quietly off stage

After a moment the living-room door opens and Frank comes in wearing a short, towelling dressing-gown over his pyjamas

He switches on the lamp UR, *blinking as his eyes adjust to the light. He goes wearily across the living-room and into the kitchen. There is the sound of the fridge door opening, a glass of milk being poured, and then the fridge door is shut. Frank comes back into the living-room. He drinks some milk and puts the glass down on the desk. He goes to the hi-fi and selecting a record from the rack, puts it on the turntable and switches it on. The Vivaldi "Concerto for Three Violins and Orchestra, in F Major", plays very softly. Frank goes to the desk, sits down, and switches on the lamp. He opens a drawer, looking for something. He pulls out a bottle of tablets, looks at them in mild surprise, and puts them back. He finds a pocket calculator and takes it out. He listens to the music a moment, trying to relax. He frees his neck and rolls his head through three hundred and sixty degrees. He picks up a pen and, using the calculator, starts scribbling figures on a pad with concentration*

The living-room door opens and Sarah comes in, wearing a dressing-gown. She closes the door behind her

Frank quickly pushes the calculator to one side

Sarah Vivaldi and milk again. What's the matter?
Frank Couldn't sleep. It was the curry. (*He taps the indigestion area of his chest*)
Sarah You hardly ate any. I watched you. Three lagers on top of that Scotch. No wonder you can't sleep.
Frank (*putting the pad face down*) You were talking in your sleep.
Sarah What were you doing? (*She tries to glance at the pad and sees the calculator*)
Frank Diagrams—for an Apically Repositioned Flap. I've some difficult surgery to do tomorrow.
Sarah With a calculator? You're lying. You were doing sums.
Frank Yes.
Sarah I thought we'd worked all those out.
Frank Not this one.
Sarah What is it?
Frank Twenty per cent of seventy thousand pounds per month. A bridging-loan.
Sarah But . . .
Frank Mr Martin called this evening. It wasn't a lab technician.
Sarah Why didn't you tell me?
Frank I wanted you to enjoy your dinner. He gave us till Friday to exchange contracts on his flat.
Sarah But that's impossible.
Frank That's what I told him. He says he's got someone else who wants to buy it.
Sarah He's bluffing.
Frank He might not be. That sort of flat's easier to sell than a big, old house.
Sarah But he promised . . .
Frank I don't blame him. We've buggered him around for months.
Sarah That's not our fault.

Frank He doesn't care whose fault it is. He's being pressed by the people he's buying from who are presumably being pressed by the people they're buying from. It's this damn daisy chain again.

Sarah starts pacing

Sarah That's the stupid English system. Can I turn that off? I feel like the recitative in an opera. (*She turns off the hi-fi*) In America you put down ten per cent deposit right away. If you back out you lose it. That stops people messing about.

Frank We're not selling our house in America.

Sarah If one of today's people made us an offer . . .

Frank Even if they did they can't possibly exchange contracts with us by Friday. There's surveyors and mortgages and Christ knows what. It can take months.

Sarah Damn it. I prayed this wouldn't happen. (*She picks up his pad, and looks at it*) One-thousand-one-hundred-and-sixty pounds. What's that for?

Frank That's what we'd pay the bank *per month* on a bridging-loan.

Sarah I don't believe it. That's over two-hundred-and-fifty pounds a week.

Frank And we'll still be paying the mortgage here.

Sarah We can't do it.

Frank Well, we wouldn't have to borrow all the money till completion.

Sarah God, I hate that word. It sounds like some sort of perversion. They were practising completion! How long can we delay *that*?

Frank It's usually six weeks or so after the exchange.

Sarah So if no-one buys this house . . .

Frank We'd go broke.

She sits down, then gets up again and paces

Sarah Oh hell, I wish I'd never seen that blasted flat. I know we're never going to find another one like it. The right size. In the right place. With a garden. I couldn't bear spending another year looking all over again.

Frank seems to have retired from the fray. She notices this

Could *you* bear that?

Frank No.

Sarah You moaned and groaned the whole time we looked.

Frank I might moan a bit when we're bankrupt.

She takes his milk and has a mouthful

There's more in the fridge. Why don't you get your own?

Sarah God, I'm forty-three . . .

Frank Happy birthday.

Sarah Very funny. You always say that.

Frank You're always saying you're forty-three. You're not unique. I've met a lot of women who are forty-three. At least I think they are. They don't keep telling me. I'm forty-seven.

Sarah Yes, and you've got a decent, fulfilling job.

Frank Oh yes! Peering into open mouths, fighting past bad breath—and all the time their terrified eyes following my every move, convinced I'm going to hurt them, on purpose.

Sarah Come on. You enjoy the teaching part. At least you're doing something worthwhile. Preserving the nation's teeth.

Frank You used to say you were helping preserve the English language —that we're both holding rot at bay.

Sarah But you get a decent salary and recognition for it. You've got professional status. I'm still just a bloody amateur.

Frank I'm sorry about that.

Sarah And you don't have to wander round an empty house all day.

Frank I thought they paid you to read manuscripts.

Sarah Paid! Ten quid to wade through one, and make a full report. And most of it's futile and filthy. The futile stuff's depressing, and the really filthy stuff I feel I ought to recommend so the publishers could make some money out of it. (*She picks up a sheaf of pages from a manuscript on the desk*) This one's about a sexually-depraved librarian in Newcastle. Read some of that. (*She puts the pages on the desk*)

Frank Must I?

Sarah It's very well written. Sometimes I feel I've wasted the last ten years.

Frank I know. On me—your children—your home—your sick father.

Sarah That's right. It's my turn now. I'm going to get some milk. (*She goes into the kitchen and there is the sound of the fridge door opening and milk being poured*)

Frank picks up the pages she has discarded and starts to read it with interest. He picks up a few more, switches off the desk lamp and crosses to the kitchen archway

Frank If it's all demented rubbish like this. I can't see what difference going and doing it in a publisher's office will make.

There is the sound of the fridge door closing

Sarah At least I'll be working with other people, not stuck here wondering whether I should start the cleaning again or get that wretched fan repaired. (*She comes out with a glass of milk*) They will only keep that job open for another month. I want this moving convulsion over by then. (*She sits down gloomily on the sofa and drinks some milk*)

Frank chucks the manuscript pages down on the coffee-table and takes his turn pacing

Frank I know. I know. It's just the worst bloody time to sell a house.

Sarah Well we're not going to give up now. The market's got to pick up soon. Oh damn it, we'll have to let the flat go.

Frank I love arguing with you. You argue both sides which covers whether I agree or disagree. (*He sits down*)

Sarah One of us has to make a decision.

Frank How can we make a decision? It doesn't depend on us, unless we
give the house away—with a free tankful of petrol.

Sarah We'll just have to see if anyone makes an offer tomorrow. (*She
clears the glasses and takes them to the kitchen*)

Frank That's the point we started all this from.

Sarah (*coming out of the kitchen*) We go round in circles like this every
night.

Frank Oh God, it's ten past three.

Sarah Why don't you have a sleeping-pill and go to bed?

Frank (*getting up wearily*) If I take one now I'll feel groggy in the morning.
I'm operating at eleven.

Sarah Apically whatsits? (*She goes towards the door and opens it*)

Frank (*moving over to turn off the lamp*) No. Two big Widman flaps.

Sarah You can do those backwards by now. Take half a pill.

Sarah goes out leaving the door open

Frank Do them backwards, and all their teeth fall out. (*He turns off the
lamp UR and, turning to go out, bangs into the door*) Oh, shit.

Frank goes out, shutting the door behind him

*Black-out. In the darkness there is the sound of Ben Gladwin's voice on a
tape. Here and there the English accent has a mild American overlay*

*Sarah and Frank enter during Ben's speech and sit at the table. Sarah
wears trousers and a blouse and Frank is dressed for going to the hospital
in a sober suit, white shirt and discreet tie. His suit jacket is on the back
of the chair*

Ben's voice Sorry not to have replied sooner to your letter. Life has been
busy, or, as they say here, gotten kinda pressured. The flat sounds great,
but selling the homestead sounds a real headache. Maybe you ought to
wait for Britain's economic recovery. Of course that could take as long
as the Second Coming. And I know *you* don't believe in that either.
The Community Centre still keeps me going all day and I have stepped
up my induction classes to four evenings a week.

The Lights come up on the living-room

*Sarah and Frank are eating their breakfast. On the table is a tray on which
there is a rack of toast, a packet of cornflakes, a coffee-pot and the rest of
the normal breakfast accessories. A folded copy of "The Guardian" is on
the table beside Sarah and the small, portable tape-recorder is between her
and Frank playing Ben's "letter". On the coffee-table are several folders, a
pile of official looking documents and a mounted model set of jaws. The
jaws are made of acrylic with inset teeth and the blood vessels and nerve-ends
are illustrated in very bright colours*

Reverend Hoskins says my baptism could now be arranged for next
month. I know you are cynical about all this, particularly you, Dad.

*Frank reacts with a vigorous nod. Sarah goes on eating her breakfast,
looking pained*

But I do think part of this is your congenital anti-Americanism. Maybe their use of language does sound corny to your ear, but you're confusing the words with the message— the truth behind the words. Christ spoke in parables, and in many tongues, I have spoken with Reverend Hoskins, about you both. At faith-reaction sessions, we prayed for you both. Don't sneer.

The phone rings

It is the sin of the Pharisees, remember?

Frank presses the stop-button on the tape-recorder

Sarah Saved—by the bell. (*She waits for Frank to answer the phone*)

Frank goes out of the room

(*Forced into answering the phone*) Hello . . . Oh, good morning, Mrs Fearnley. . . . Oh, good . . . Yes, by all means . . . I've got someone coming to lunch, but twelve would be fine . . . Quite . . . Quite . . . See you then. Goodbye. (*She puts the phone down*)

Frank comes back into the room with his empty briefcase

Mrs Fearnley. She wants to come back and see it again. I told you they were interested.
Frank She might just want a free coffee. Who's coming to lunch?
Sarah Liz.

Sarah crosses back to the dining-table. Frank starts to pack his briefcase. He puts his papers in, including, by mistake, the pages of Sarah's manuscript he put down there the previous evening

Frank Oh.
Sarah Do you want the end of the morning service?
Frank No. I'll save it for evensong.
Sarah Maybe if he wrote it in a letter I could accept it better. It's hearing his voice—saying those things. In Connecticut. Why does it embarrass me so much?
Frank Because you're a nice, rational *Guardian*-reader. Frankly it makes me feel a bit sick. It's so bloody sanctimonious.
Sarah I suppose he'll get over it. He got over Sanyassi Buddhism before he left.
Frank At least while he was meditating he was quiet.
Sarah You didn't have to cook vegetarian for him. Maybe we should have taken him to church more.
Frank What do you mean *more*? We never took either of them to church. And Jane's not converting to anything, as far as we know.
Sarah (*starting to clear the table but leaving her coffee-cup*) He'll come out of it soon. (*She takes the tray of breakfast things into the kitchen*)
Frank But what as? He'll probably come back here as an orthodox Jew.
Sarah (*coming back from the kitchen*) Then I'll have *more* trouble cooking for him. What time's your first appointment?

Frank Ten.
Sarah How do you feel?
Frank Not a day over eighty-five. (*He picks up his dental model to put it in his briefcase*)
Sarah You showing Jaws again today?
Frank Yes. Second-year students. The Perils of Gingivitis.
Sarah (*doing toothless impression*) Or where would we all be without dental floss?

He manages to get the model into his briefcase. Sarah crosses to the drinks cupboard, and gets out a half-empty sherry bottle. She uncorks it and starts to pour the sherry from the decanter into it

Frank (*looking across at her*) What are you doing?
Sarah My sister's coming to lunch. (*She looks at the decanter*) That should be two glasses worth.
Frank Haven't you got enough to do without having her here today?
Sarah (*putting the sherry and Scotch bottles in the lower cupboard*) Don't complain. I'm having her to lunch so you won't have to entertain her all evening. I'm going to try and be nice to her today.
Frank By hiding the booze?
Sarah She's having a bad patch at the moment.
Frank When isn't she? (*After a pause, doing up the briefcase*) Between men, I suppose.
Sarah And between therapists too. (*She takes her coffee-cup and the tape-recorder from the table to the desk*)
Frank (*going towards the door*) You know what I think's really wrong with your sister?
Sarah (*wearily*) Yes. She just needs her gums fixing. You're going to be late. (*She starts to sort the manuscripts*)
Frank Good luck with Mrs Fearnley. Don't mention your sense of direction again.
Sarah Bye.

Frank goes out, shutting the door behind him

Sarah stretches and yawns. The front door bangs and she sits lost in thought for a moment at her desk. Then she determinedly pulls a manuscript towards her and puts her glasses on. She changes her mind and rewinds the tape slightly and presses the playback-button. She takes her glasses off and listens to Ben's voice

Ben's voice I'm looking forward to the fall—autumn, here. It's meant to be beautiful in New England. The leaves go incredible colours. I'll send you a dogwood leaf. They go scarlet. God bless you.
Sarah Amen. (*There is a moment's silence. She presses the stop-button and sits thinking for a moment, then she drinks some of her lukewarm coffee. She flicks out Ben's tape and puts in a new one. She plugs in a little microphone, presses the record-button and speaks into it*) Hi, Ben. It's Mom. I've got a machine too. These days all God's children got tape-machines. I normally use mine for book-reports and send them into the

office for typing. Ben, we miss you a great deal– that is until your
monthly sermon arrives. It's hard for two lapsed C of E's to take—
over the cornflakes. Oh damn it, Ben, can't you see we don't mind
what you choose to believe, and never have? But the words do matter.
In the beginning was *the* Word, wasn't it? That's not anti-American,
is it? Do you seriously think if Jesus had sent office-memos to the
disciples we'd have ended up with the Gospels? Would the Parables
have survived if they'd been written in corporate gobbledegook? Ben,
can't you see you're being turned into an earnest, sanctimonious—
ninny? Do you have to be born again? Wasn't once enough? (*She
realizes she has got carried away, gone too far*) It's O.K., Ben. I'm not
going to send you this. (*She presses the stop-button and then the rewind
button and sits staring at the tape rewinding. She opens a desk-drawer,
gets out a bottle of Valium, unscrews the top, then changes her mind and
puts the bottle back. She presses the record-button, picks up the manuscript
and speaks into the microphone*) "Report by Sarah Gladwin on *Away
Game*. A novel by . . . (*The top page is not there*)

The phone rings

(*She stares at the phone for a moment and then answers it*) Hello . . .
Oh, Mr Goodis. Any news? . . . No. A lot came, but nobody made an
offer to us. You don't happen to know if Mr Martin has got someone
else after his flat, do you? . . . Oh, not through you. I see . . . Yes.
I'll phone you. Goodbye. (*She puts the phone down, looking depressed,
and then rests her head in her hands*) Damn it. Damn it. Damn it. (*She
opens the desk-drawer, gets out the bottle of Valium and, without thinking about it, pops a tablet into her mouth and swallows it down with
some cold coffee. She puts her glasses on and looks down at the manuscript, but then looks puzzled as the top pages are missing. She looks for
them on the desk and remembers Frank picked them up the previous
evening. She gets up and starts looking round the room's surfaces. She
acts out what he did with them, realizing he put them down on the coffee-
table, and they are not there now. It dawns on her that he has taken them
in his briefcase*) Oh, damn it. (*She shrugs, and goes back to her desk.
She glances at what's left of the manuscript, and picks up a pad of her
notes on it. She presses the record-button and, glancing at her notes,
starts to talk into the little microphone*) Report by Sarah Gladwin on
Away Game by name to follow. I have tried very hard to come to terms
with this novel. It has many virtues. It is written in clear, strong prose,
and conveys a keen sense of its time and place. For me, the problem
lies in the two levels of the story, and the relevance of one to the other.
On the one hand the erotic, surrealist fantasy, and on the other, the
day-to-day reality of a seedy, unemployed librarian in Newcastle . . .
Why, when in reality the librarian states clearly he is six foot two, do
his fantasies concern a three foot one dwarf? I realize that three foot
one is half six foot two. His dwarf is half the man he is. Very symbolic.
But in fantasy one would surely expect the hero to be twice the man he is,
except, of course, you couldn't have a twelve foot, four inch dwarf.

Black-out

Sarah exits taking the coffee-cup with her

In the darkness Sarah's voice is heard on tape

Sarah's voice Perhaps I have missed something, and am being unfair to the author.

The Lights come up on an empty living-room. The table now has a cold lunch laid out on it—two plates of tuna salad and a plate of rolls

The door opens, and Sarah comes in with her sister, Liz. Liz is about four years younger than Sarah, and, in manner and appearance, is almost a complete antithesis of her. She is more made-up, and her hair has a carefully contrived unkempt look. She wears expensive, up-market jeans, an ethnic blouse and carries a short, fur jacket and holdall. Everything about her is slightly over-stated, over-dramatic

Sarah Where are you going?
Liz Here.

She puts her holdall down near the door. Sarah's expression is the opposite of warm welcome

Sarah But I thought you were just coming for lunch.
Liz I only want to stay for a couple of days, while they finish painting my flat.
Sarah You're having it painted *again*?
Liz Since David left I can't bear it there. It depresses me. I thought I'd change the colours, move the furniture round a bit.
Sarah You might at least have warned me.
Liz I thought, you've got a big, empty house you can't get rid of . . .
Sarah Damn it, Liz . . . (*Checking herself*) It's a bad time. There'll be people coming to look at the house.
Liz I'll be out all day. I'm rehearsing.
Sarah Lunch is ready.
Liz (*going over and looking at the lunch laid out on the table*) You're still the best-organized person I know. Not tuna-fish salad again. Let's have a drink. (*She comes back, sits on the sofa, takes her cigarettes from her handbag and lights one*)
Sarah Ah! We only seem to have a very little sherry left. Or there are some—

Liz glances at the almost empty decanter and smiles, as though this is an old ritual

Sarah }
                 } (*together*) { —sticky liqueurs . . .
Liz   }   { Sticky liqueurs that patients give Frank as presents.

Sarah looks away quickly, embarrassed to have been caught out

Liz A sherry would be fine. (*She goes over and unzips her holdall. She takes out two bottles of white wine and holds them out to Sarah*) To go with lunch.

Sarah One bottle each?

Liz No. One's for tomorrow.

Sarah Don't you mean tonight?

Liz No. I've got to go out tonight. I'll put this in the fridge. (*She puts one bottle on the dining-table and takes the other to the kitchen*)

Sarah pours two glasses of sherry as Liz comes back from the kitchen

Sarah What are you rehearsing?

Liz A telly. One of those endless courtroom dramas.

Sarah Is it a good part?

Liz Not bad. There were two women's parts. A barrister and a shop-lifter who drinks. Guess the casting. Cheers. (*She drinks*)

Sarah Cheers. (*She drinks*)

Liz wanders over to the desk and glances at the heap of manuscripts

Liz Read any good books lately?

Sarah No.

Liz Poor dears. They're all going to be so disappointed. I'm not sure I could sit in judgement like that.

Sarah is clearly nettled by Liz's fairly constant implied criticism

Sarah I'm not judging them. I'm only judging whether my employers should publish them or not.

Liz Who writes them all?

Sarah Sometimes it seems like half the population. A lot of it is home therapy—cheaper than paying an analyst.

Liz (*going and sitting on the sofa*) You mean I should write a book.

Sarah No. Unless you want to.

Liz stubs out her cigarette and looks from her empty sherry-glass to the empty decanter

Liz No. Let's open a bottle of wine. (*She goes to the dining-table*)

Sarah (*taking the empty sherry glasses*) All right. I'll get the corkscrew. Let's eat. I've still got a lot of reading to do this afternoon (*She goes into the kitchen*) How was Mum?

Liz O.K. Managing.

Sarah I phoned her last week. How long did you stay?

Liz A couple of days. (*She opens the plastic lid on the wine bottle*)

Sarah comes out of the kitchen with the corkscrew

Sarah We've been trying to get down there for ages.

Sarah goes to get wine-glasses from the drinks cupboard at the same time as Liz is pouring the wine into the water tumblers

But we're still showing people round here. (*She comes back with the wine-glasses*)

Liz Nobody interested yet? (*She takes her plate to the sofa, ignoring the place-settings*)

Sarah There was a woman meant to come at twelve. She never showed up. Would you rather eat there?
Liz Yes, fine.

Sarah gets a tray from the kitchen and puts the lunch things on it

But you're still going to move to that flat?
Sarah If it's humanly possible, yes. (*She brings the full tray to join Liz at the sofa and places the tray on the coffee-table*)
Liz Well, you're lucky Mum's happy with Aunt Sophie.
Sarah Yes. Why are *we* lucky?

Liz drinks, while Sarah starts eating

Liz You can sell your house and move to something smaller. No need for a granny flat. Most couples get rid of one lot of kids, breathe a sigh of relief, and suddenly find they've got another lot to look after— ageing parents.
Sarah And what about you?

Liz drinks at twice Sarah's speed

Liz I didn't have kids, did I? (*She starts to eat*)
Sarah No, but you've got an ageing parent.
Liz If anything happened she wouldn't want to come and live with me.

She refills Sarah's glass, merely a token as Sarah has hardly drunk any, and then refills her own almost empty glass. They go on eating

Sarah That's because you're careful only to have one bed.
Liz She wouldn't come to me because we've never liked each other enough.
Sarah I don't think it necessarily depends on that.
Liz That's what my dear ex-husband used to say.
Sarah Yes, I can imagine John saying that.
Liz If I'd listened to him I'd have ended up as your twin.

Sarah is about to reply but she drinks instead

I know you and Frank disapproved of me getting divorced.
Sarah Look, I don't ask you what you think of my marriage. I don't think it matters what we think of your divorce.
Liz Or my living with a married man with two kids?
Sarah You brought David here. We were perfectly pleasant to him. And all the others. Why do you suddenly want our approval?
Liz I don't really. It's just that I sometimes feel like one of those manu- scripts sitting here waiting to be judged by your rigid high standards.
Sarah Utter nonsense. That's all in your mind, not mine.
Liz Is it? I always feel I have to watch my language when I'm here.
Sarah Rubbish.
Liz I bet when you and Frank fight you say "damn" and "blast" and never "shit" and "fuck". Maybe sometimes Frank says "bugger".
Sarah Sometimes I wonder why he doesn't tell you to bugger-off when you're getting at him.

Liz I think it's because he fancies me, deep down beneath his molars.
Sarah He's always kept it very secret, if he does. (*She clears the plates and goes out into the kitchen*)

Liz refills her glass. Drink clearly relaxes her physically and verbally

Liz I used to have fantasies about Frank, all stern in his white coat, and me in the chair . . .

Sarah comes out of the kitchen with a board of cheese and comes back to the sofa

Sarah You're doing what you did at sixteen. You're trying to shock people.
Liz No, not people. Just you—and Mum. Dr Kramer said I'd so identified you with Mum that my reactions to you both were virtually the same.
Sarah Have a roll.
Liz Dr Kramer's an expert on sibling rivalry, you see. He says that you always got your own way, set the standards. So I went the other way, not to risk odious comparisons. You went to college, so I didn't.
Sarah I thought you just failed the exams.
Liz No. Subconsciously on purpose.
Sarah Ah!
Liz You married young. So I didn't. Then, at thirty, I panicked. Not much of a career, no husband. Felt left-out. Married a doctor because you'd married a dentist . . .

Sarah drinks some more wine. She seems suddenly relaxed, and content to let Liz rattle on

For a while I accepted your standards, gave up everything . . . What's the matter?

She peers at Sarah, realizing she is listening calmly with unusual attentiveness

Sarah Matter?
Liz You're not fighting back.
Sarah No.
Liz Why not?
Sarah After a Valium and some wine you don't seem quite so impossible.
Liz I didn't know you took Valium.
Sarah I never took anything like that—not till we started this moving business. Go on.
Liz Go on?
Sarah Yes. It's very interesting.
Liz Because it's all about you.
Sarah Yes. Maybe that's it. I could never afford an analyst. We were too busy paying school-fees. If we'd sent them to the local comprehensive I could have afforded an analyst. I suppose it's very middle-class to put one's children's education first.

Liz Oh, you've never needed an analyst. You've always been in control.
Sarah In control? With the kids? This house? Frank's career? You're
joking. That's why I want to move. So I can get control again before
it's too late. Why did you give up Dr Kramer?

The doorbell rings

Who can that be? It can't be that woman about the house.

*Sarah puts her glass on the floor, gets up and goes out to the hall to open
the front door*

Liz drinks some more wine and puts her glass on the tray

*There is the sound of the front door opening and Sarah greeting Beryl
Fearnley*

(*Off*) Oh, good afternoon, Mrs Fearnley.
Beryl (*off*) I'm terribly sorry I'm late.

*At the sound of the following chat from the hall Liz is galvanized into action.
She races across the room, grabs her jacket and her holdall, and rushes to
dump them in the kitchen, en route noticing the remains of the lunch things
on the table. She comes out of the kitchen, and, at breakneck speed, takes
the tray and races back into the kitchen where she puts on the short, fur
jacket over her blouse and jeans, a long, silk scarf round her neck, and a pair
of dark glasses*

Sarah (*off*) Don't worry about that. Come in.

The front door closes

Beryl (*off*) Had a puncture—took my bike to the repair shop . . . I should
have phoned, but I couldn't find a phone that wasn't vandalized . . .
Do hope you haven't waited in for me.
Sarah (*off*) Oh no, of course not.

*Sarah comes into the room with Beryl who wears another flowing and
flung-together ensemble. She is even more flustered and fluttery than on
her last visit*

Beryl It's really only the kitchen I wanted to see again. And the garden
in the daytime. I do hope I'm not putting you out.
Sarah No, no. Not at all. I was just finishing my lunch. (*She registers
that the lunch has totally disappeared*)

Liz sweeps grandly out of the kitchen

Liz It's a wonderful kitchen, Mrs Gladwin. And I really love—the
garden. (*She stops, taking in Beryl*)

Sarah glances at Liz, stunned to silence

Beryl Oh dear, I'm sorry. I've interrupted you.
Liz No. *I'm* sorry. I've been here far too long already. It's just that one
rarely sees such a lovely house.

Sarah stops Liz over-acting

Sarah This is Mrs Fearnley . . .

Liz How do you do? I'm Mrs Smith. Mrs Gladwin, while you're showing Mrs Fearnley round in here, might I have another look upstairs?

Sarah (*wearily*) Yes.

Liz Thank you so much. I do so wish my husband was here too. He's at a meeting in New York at the moment but he'll be back tomorrow morning.

Liz smiles graciously at Beryl and goes out

Embarrassed, Sarah smiles at Beryl

Beryl Please, I'm the one who's late. If you'd like to go round with her . . .

Sarah No, no. She knows her way round . . . She's been here for hours. Why don't you look round the kitchen—and the garden. I'm afraid it's all a bit of a mess today.

She gestures Beryl into the kitchen. She stands, gathering herself, and notices her half-full glass and the bottle of wine on the floor by the coffee-table. She rushes over to get it, but then clearly doesn't want to appear in the kitchen with it. She looks for somewhere to hide it. It is a blank moment. She can't think where to put it where it won't be seen. She decides on the lower drinks cupboard, goes there, takes a tiny sip, and puts the bottle and glass in. Beryl comes out as Sarah straightens up guiltily

Beryl It's a beautiful kitchen, and the garden looks lovely.

Sarah Would you like to look upstairs again?

Baryl No. I don't want to bother you. I remember it all. Anyway, I'm sure you'd like to finish with Mrs Smith.

Sarah Mrs Smith?

Beryl Finish off showing her around.

Sarah Oh yes. No. She'll be fine.

Beryl John—my husband loved the house too. He tried to phone our friends last night to tell them we had found something. (*She talks in short nervous bursts, her eyes wandering around the room, taking in details*) They were out last night. So he's speaking to them today. He didn't want to make a serious offer till he'd spoken to them. He's very proper that way, a lot of people aren't these days. They'd have to sell their house too. Our friends in Skegness, I mean. But it's probably not so hard in Skegness.

Sarah no longer seems to have the energy to cut into Beryl's breathless flow as Beryl unwittingly backs her up against the desk

They've only got one child, so our house is ideal for them. It was fine for us when we only had two. But since Jenny, well, since she got bigger —she's our youngest—she's nine now. We have four, you see. Oh, I told you that last night. It's been terribly difficult. It's far too small. We've looked and looked for something bigger. I thought we'd found something six months ago, but then the people decided not to sell. John got furious. And gave up looking. So I've gone on—on my own. It's been exhausting. I saw your house was on the market four months ago. But it was a little beyond our price range then.

Sarah seems mesmerized by her, and is now up against the desk, trapped

Sarah Yes, well . . .

Beryl But since you brought it down though—well, I persuaded John to come and look at it. He's been so busy recently. In the office. You know, all these education cuts, he's—oh, dear. (*She stops in mid-sentence, as though a catastrophic thought has hit her. She looks crestfallen*) Oh dear, I'm sorry. I'm so sorry.

Sarah Sorry? What about?

Beryl (*looking quite drained and moving guiltily away from Sarah*) I'm talking too much. I know I do it. I can hear myself doing it. I suppose it's being on my own all day now. John says I ought to get a job—even a part-time one—be with people. But it's easy for him to say that.

Sarah I know what you mean. I talk to myself sometimes.

Beryl But at least you have work to do. I mean you have to read. I used to read a lot, I even used to go to French conversation classes, but—a small house gets into such a mess with four kids. I seem to spend all day cleaning it. I know it's silly, but when one . . .

Sarah No. I'm sure we all do that. It's a bit easier in a big house. When my children were here, we just shut doors on the mess.

Beryl Of course, your children are off now. That must feel strange. At least mine still come home every evening.

Sarah Yes, one seems to have devoted most of one's life to one's children and one's home. Then suddenly . . . yes it does feel strange.

There is a sudden silence. Beryl is inwardly struggling not to talk, and yet clearly doesn't want to leave. Sarah suddenly seems to share Beryl's depression

Would you like a drink?

Beryl Oh—I shouldn't stay . . .

Sarah I'm sure you need one. I know what hell house-hunting is. Sherry?

Beryl Just a small one.

Sarah Do sit down. (*She gets down the sherry bottle out of the cupboard, pours a glass and puts the bottle back*)

Beryl (*sitting on the sofa*) Thank you.

Sarah I read somewhere that the three most traumatic things that happen to ordinary people are bereavement, divorce and moving house. (*Sarah hands the glass of sherry to Beryl*)

Beryl Thank you. Aren't you having one?

Sarah No. I had one before lunch. If I have more, I'll sleep all afternoon, and I've some reading to do.

Beryl Cheers then.

Liz breezes in

Liz The upstairs is perfect. (*Noticing Beryl's glass*) Sherry! How nice!

Sarah Yes, well. You've seen everything now, twice.

Liz I'll persuade my husband to come and see it when he gets back from New York. Or was it Geneva?

Sarah No, New York.

Liz Oh yes. It's so seldom one sees such a well-kept house, isn't it, Mrs Fearnley?
Beryl Yes, it is.
Sarah With people dropping in unexpectedly . . .

Liz goes and sits next to Beryl on the sofa. Sarah looks furious

Liz It looks as though it's always terribly tidy. I've been looking for months for something with five bedrooms.
Beryl Yes. I have too.
Liz It's so nice to find a spacious house that isn't impossible to run.
Sarah Yes. Well, I'm glad you like it. Now if you've seen everything you want . . .
Liz Oh yes, I have. I'm sure my husband will like it too. He's terribly fussy about bathrooms. He'll love the one *en suite.*
Sarah Well, if you get your husband back, do bring him round.
Liz Yes, I will.
Sarah I don't want you to be—late for your next appointment.
Liz That's all right. After this I don't want to see any more houses.
Sarah No, I meant the hospital.
Liz The hospital?
Sarah Yes, you told me your mother was very ill in hospital, and visiting hours were only from two to three. It's two now.
Liz Oh, yes.
Sarah I'm sure your mother must look forward to seeing you, especially if she's so ill.
Liz Yes. My poor mother.
Beryl Oh, I am sorry. Is she very ill?
Liz Yes. In fact she doesn't really recognize me now, so it's hardly worth going to see her at all.
Sarah Well maybe today she will recognize you. You *must* go.
Beryl I do hope your mother gets better.
Sarah Yes. So do I. (*She advances, taking Liz's arm firmly*)
Liz (*taking her handbag*) Thank you so much for showing me around, Mrs Gladwin.
Sarah You're very welcome. Just give me a little warning before you come again.
Liz Goodbye, Mrs Fearnley. There's no need to show me out. I can find the front door.

Liz looks daggers at Sarah and goes out through the front door

Beryl I hope I didn't interfere—being late . . .
Sarah No. She'd been here for ages.
Beryl She seemed to like the house.
Sarah Yes—well. I'm sure she behaves like that at every house she sees. In fact she told me, before you came, that her husband really wants to live in the country.
Beryl Oh—oh good. Now I must let you get on. (*She gets up*) You've

been very kind. We do love your house. I'm sure my husband will—I mean he won't make an offer unless he means to go through with it.

Sarah No, I quite understand.

Beryl I only hope—you can wait. Could you wait? Just another day or so?

Sarah Well, we are under pressure to exchange contracts, but I don't think another day will make any difference.

Beryl You're very kind. You will give us one more day then?

Sarah Yes, of course.

Beryl I'm so glad you've found a place that you like. I mustn't take up any more of your time. I'm sorry I talked so much. It's just this dreadful house-hunting . . .

Beryl and Sarah go out to the hall

Sarah (*off*) Goodbye.

The front door shuts

Sarah comes back into the living-room and takes a deep breath

She crosses and picks up the empty sherry glass, groans to herself, and puts the glass down by the decanter

Liz, having come in through the back door, enters from the kitchen

Liz Thank you. You practically slung me out. All that nonsense about Mother in hospital.

Sarah Well, you asked for it.

Liz Asked for it? After all I did?

Sarah You made the poor woman feel terrible.

Liz takes her dark glasses and jacket off

Liz God, you're thick sometimes, Sarah. Don't you see? She'll go home and tell her husband that some—

Sarah That some loony woman was wandering round the house.

Liz That some rich, fascinating woman was crazy about the house and her husband is coming from Geneva.

Sarah New York.

Liz That's what they need—some real competition to get them going.

Sarah Look, it was a lovely audition, dear, but Mrs Fearnley's sold on the house already. It's her husband who's the stumbling-block. (*Looking at her watch*) Oh, Lord, is that the time? I've got to get through this manuscript today.

Liz I can take a hint.

Sarah Thanks for clearing up anyway.

Liz I'm going up to my room. I'm exhausted after that performance. I've always hated matinées.

Liz goes out

Sarah crosses to her desk, sits down and, stifling a huge yawn, pulls a new pile of manuscripts towards her. She tries to read, shifting in her seat, drowsy and uncomfortable. She takes the manuscript over to the sofa, props herself up and starts to read with the pile of pages on her lap

Sarah Oh no, not one of those. Not firm, round breasts again. (*Reading aloud*) "Her firm, round buttocks pressed against the paddle . . ." paddle? . . . oh, "saddle . . ." (*She flips over several pages*) ". . . she sank on to the bed, shut her eyes, and felt the warmth of his . . ." (*The effect of wine, Valium, Liz and Mrs Fearnley, starts to take effect. Sarah's head lolls forward. She jerks it back, trying hard to read. It slumps again. This time she gives in, and drops off. She moves slightly into a more comfortable position. The pages of the manuscript in her lap cascade to the floor but but she is too weary to do anything about it, as she drifts into a deep sleep*)

The Lights fade to Black-out and then come up again

(*She is now in a more comfortable, deep sleep position on the sofa, the manuscript still scattered on the floor*)

Frank comes in, just back from work, carrying his briefcase. He stares at the comatose Sarah, puts his briefcase down on a chair, skirts round the scattered manuscript, and goes to the drinks cupboard. He reaches in to pull out a bottle of Scotch, and discovers the half-drunk glass of wine that Sarah hid in there. He looks at it, and then at Sarah and the manuscript on the floor. He frowns, and puts the glass back. He pours himself a large Scotch, rattling the glass against the bottle

(*Waking up with a start and staring at Frank*) What are you doing here?
Frank I live here. Unless of course you've sold it today. Any—er—anyone offer?
Sarah No. What time is it?
Frank Nearly six.

Sarah looks at the pages on the floor, then shakes her head to clear it of sleep

Sarah Heavens, I've slept for hours. You had a good day?
Frank No. Boring story? (*He sits down wearily on the sofa, and drinks some Scotch*)
Sarah (*picking up the manuscript*) Very. By the way, those pages you were looking at last night . . .
Frank Which pages?
Sarah The sex-crazed librarian. (*She indicates the coffee-table*) You put them down on that table, didn't you? (*She puts the manuscript back on the desk*)
Frank Yes. I think so.
Sarah That's what I thought. You must have picked them up with your papers this morning. I need them. The poor author's going to want them back.
Frank I gave all those papers to my secretary. It was the piece on plaque control for the *Dental Journal*.
Sarah Well, for heaven's sake get them back tomorrow.
Frank Well, I hope she saw them and realized . . .

The phone rings

Sarah I'm going to start making supper. (*She moves from the desk and goes into the kitchen*)

Frank goes and answers the phone

Frank (*into the phone*) Hello . . . Yes. Oh, Mr Goodis, hello . . .

At the sound of the name Sarah comes out of the kitchen. She stays tensely in the archway, listening to the conversation

. . . An offer. Good. Who? . . . Ah, yes. How much? . . . How do I know that's genuine? . . . Yes. Ask my solicitor . . . You're sure Mr Martin won't let us go beyond Friday? . . . Yes, I see . . . Yes. No, fine. I'll call you first thing in the morning . . . Thanks. Goodbye. (*He puts the phone down*)

Sarah (*excitedly*) An offer?

Frank Yes. Eighty-five.

Sarah But that's four thousand less than . . .

Frank No-one offers the asking price these days—even when you've just slashed it.

Sarah And Mr Martin won't wait?

Frank No. He can't. He loses *his* house if he does.

Sarah Then we'll have to accept it. I knew the Fearnleys would come through. She was determined . . .

Frank No. It's the Bellings.

Sarah The Bellings! I won't sell to them. I hated them. I don't want them in here.

Frank But they're cash-buyers.

Sarah (*sarcastically*) Oh, yes.

Frank Now. Look. Goodis said we can ask them to prove it to our solicitor, so I'll call Laurence, and ask him to look at their lease. And they've promised to get a surveyor in fast.

Sarah I don't care. We can't sell to them.

Frank Are you crazy? We're desperate.

Sarah I promised Mrs Fearnley we'd wait at least twenty-four hours for her offer.

Frank takes a swig of his drink, trying to suppress his fury. Sarah goes to the kitchen to prepare supper. They shout between the living-room and kitchen

Frank Oh, you did, did you? Like you promised the Davidsons and the Cullens. The bloody Fearnleys are more of the same.

Sarah They have friends who want to buy their house.

Frank And their friends have a house to sell too, don't they? And you think Fearnley won't mess us around forever? He's a Civil Servant, isn't he? Department of Education. They change their bloody minds every ten minutes about how to teach our kids maths.

Sarah I would rather trust the Fearnleys.

Frank It's not a question of trust. It's a question of the Fearnleys' unknown friends selling *their* house.

Sarah They're in Skegness.

Frank Oh really. Living in a field, I suppose. Or on a park-bench?

Sarah Maybe it's easier to sell a house up there.

Frank Oh? Has there been an economic miracle in Skegness? They've struck oil? Banned Japanese car imports?

Sarah (*coming out of the kitchen with a chopping knife*) Mrs Fearnley was here this afternoon. And I felt very sorry for her. She's going through exactly what I went through five years ago—only with twice as many children and in a smaller house. I feel she has more right to live here than those . . .

Frank No-one has a right to live any place anymore. Will you please understand we're selling a house, not making a donation to the Women's Movement.

Sarah You have no feelings. About people—about a home. We've lived here for fourteen years. We've made it the way it is. Don't you care who lives in it now?

Frank (*standing close to Sarah, shouting*) No. I used to—six months ago. Now I don't care if it's turned into a sauna and massage parlour.

Sarah You've got bad breath.

Frank I'm not surprised. I've been too bloody tired to clean my teeth for a week. Don't you understand we can't be sentimental about it? It's business. The bank manager isn't going to be sentimental about a bridging-loan. And you want that flat, don't you?

Sarah The house is half mine, and I will not sell it to the Bellings.

Frank (*in a fury*) Oh fine. Then you sell your half to the Fearnleys. I'll sell my half to the Bellings. We'll let them fight over it.

Sarah (*turning her back on him and heading for the door*) Well if you're suddenly in charge, you can make your own damn supper for a start.

She storms out, banging the door

Frank looks at his glass which is empty. He goes and pours himself another

Frank is still furious when the door opens and Liz comes in. She has changed her jeans for other trousers and has her fur jacket on. She carries some shopping

Frank looks at her in surprise

Liz Hello. What's the matter with Sarah?

Frank You're a bit late for lunch, aren't you?

Liz We had lunch ages ago. I've been out shopping since then. Didn't Sarah tell you I was here?

Frank No.

Liz You look like you've had a hard day at the office.

Frank The office was all right. It was when I got home . . .

Liz Oh good. You *were* fighting.

Frank Sarah was just telling me who is and isn't good enough to buy our house. I was crass enough to think that money might be a qualification.

Liz Poor loves. You're under strain, that's all. The director I'm working
for on my telly has just been trying to sell his house. Been trying for a
year.

Frank That's encouraging. We've only been at it four months.

Liz He got struck with two houses, enormous bank loan. Then his
marriage broke up, so he's paying his wife alimony. Now she lives in the
new house, while he's trying to sell the old house, so he can buy a cheap
bed-sit somewhere.

Frank I'm so glad you told me that.

Liz I was just trying to help you be philosophic.

Frank Thanks.

Liz There are people worse off than you, you know. You'll be all right.

Frank Yes?

Liz Yes. You and Sarah always end up all right. Cheer up, or I'll ask
your advice about this new bridge my dentist wants to give me.

Frank I've cheered up. You're—er—not staying for supper, are you?

Liz No. I have to go out. I must go and change.

Frank Ah. Well, enjoy yourself.

Liz Thanks. And don't wait up for me.

Frank Wait up for you?

Liz I've got a key.

Frank What?

Liz I'm staying for a couple of nights while they're painting my flat.

Liz goes out

*Frank stands for a moment, looking baffled. He takes another mouthful of
his drink. He squares his shoulders and crosses determinedly to the phone.
He picks it up and dials*

Frank Hello, Laurence . . . It's Frank . . . Gladwin. Sorry to bother you
at home. It's just there's been developments here. I'm going to accept
an offer from some people called Belling . . . They say they're cash-
buyers. Lease up on their flat. I gather it's in order for you to get them
to prove it . . . If you could. We'll go through with exchanging contracts
with Martin on Friday . . . (*Listening to a lecture*) . . . I know a bridging-
loan would be suicide. It's a toss-up between suicide or divorce. Maybe
suicide would be the cheapest way out. After all I am a dentist. I could
gas myself. We're selling to the Bellings.

The Lights fade to Black-out

Frank exits and Sarah and Joan Belling enter

The Lights come up on the living-room

*Sarah stands by the sofa with a cup of coffee, looking none too happy. Joan,
in a flashy, trendy outfit, is measuring curtains with a steel tape-measure in
the bay*

Joan Of course, my husband's so busy at the moment with recording
sessions. He didn't want to move at all at this point. Wanted us to stay
in a hotel for a while.

Sarah Wouldn't that have been rather expensive?

Joan We could have charged it to the company. But our kids would have hated it.

Sarah How old are they?

Joan Seven and five. It would have meant an extra suite for them. And for the Nanny. It's awful how nothing you've got fits, isn't it?

Sarah Well, we could arrange to leave those behind, if you like.

Joan That's very kind of you but—(*examining the curtains*)—I think we'll get new ones.

There is the sound of banging from upstairs. Sarah looks up worriedly

That must be Peter in the loft. He just wanted to see if we could use it. He'd like to make a big sound studio up there. (*She goes over and measures the bay window*) How are the neighbours here?

Sarah We've found them fine.

Joan Are they young or old?

Sarah Depends where you draw the line. On that side they're our age— with three children. Over there—slightly older.

Liz comes in. She wears old jeans, a sloppy tee-shirt, and is clearly not long out of bed, after a bad night. She doesn't notice Joan measuring in the bay window

Liz Sarah. There's some maniac banging around on my ceiling.

Sarah It's Mr Belling.

Liz Who?

Sarah gestures at Joan. Liz finally registers her

Sarah The Bellings are buying the house. This is Mrs Belling. This is my sister.

Liz Oh. Hello.

Joan How do you do? I'm sorry if my husband disturbed you.

Liz That's all right. I just thought it was a migraine attack. (*She looks into the cup Sarah is holding*) Coffee?

Sarah There's some in the kitchen.

Liz goes into the kitchen

Sarah puts her coffee cup down on the desk. Joan is now inspecting the carpet

Joan This carpet? Do you know what's under it?

Sarah The floor. I mean, you know, floor-boards.

Joan I thought parquet would look nice in here. We've got some nice rugs to put down on it.

Peter Belling comes in. He looks very sharp in a business-suit and a colourful open-necked shirt

Peter That's a big loft. Make a great studio. Big job to convert. Mean knocking the whole top floor through. Very expensive.

Joan That's your department.

Peter Did my wife tell you—my surveyor said he could manage to come on Friday?

Sarah Friday.

Peter This Friday. Luckily I know him pretty well, or it would have been a three week wait. I know you're in a hurry though. You want to exchange on your new place, don't you?

Sarah Yes.

Peter When do you have to do that?

Sarah Friday.

Peter Oh! Well I'm sure he'll get the report to me in a couple of days. We should be all set by early next week.

Joan All these formalities are so boring, aren't they?

Sarah Yes.

Peter Come on. I'm going to be late for that recording session. Thanks very much, Mrs Gladwin.

Joan Thank you. I'll phone you about when I want to come back. I thought I might let a kitchen-designer see what he could do.

Sarah (*sourly*) Fine.

Sarah shows Peter and Joan out to the front door

Liz comes out of the kitchen with her cup of coffee

Sarah comes back into the living-room looking gloomy

Liz So it's really all happening?

Sarah Yes.

Liz You don't look very happy about it.

Sarah I'm not. (*She takes her empty coffee-cup from the desk and goes and sits on the sofa. She is about to finish her coffee and then realizes it's empty*) You spend fourteen years making a home, and then—oh hell, I suppose it's just me. I hate their manners and their music, and she hates my curtains, carpets and kitchen.

The Lights fade slowly to Black-out

Sarah and Liz exit with the coffee-cups

In the darkness the voices of Frank, Sarah and Laurence, the Gladwins' solicitor, are heard on tape. Laurence has a rather dry, precise voice which gives the sequence the feel of a solemn wedding-ceremony

Laurence's voice . . . and it's for nine-hundred-and-ninety-seven years. You're both read the contract for the flat through carefully?

Frank's voice Yes.

Sarah's voice Yes.

Laurence's voice Is there any part you want me to explain?

Frank's voice No.

Sarah's voice No.

Laurence's voice Mr Martin's giving you six weeks to completion, so let's hope these Belling people turn up trumps. (*Pause*) Right, well, you both sign here . . .

Sarah's voice Here? Yes.
Laurence's voice And Frank signs below you . . . Good. And again here
. . . and here . . . and here. And here, and here.

The Lights come up on the living-room

*Peter Belling comes into the living-room. He wears well-pressed jeans
and a coloured sports shirt. Frank follows him in, wearing his casual
weekend clothes*

Peter I'm sorry to come at such short notice, but there's a couple of things
come up we ought to discuss.
Frank Do sit down, my wife will be back in a moment and she'll make us
some tea. In fact why don't I put the kettle on now? (*He goes into the
kitchen*)

*Peter casts his eye round the room. He goes and looks at the cracks over the
door and then gets the notebook from his pocket. As Frank goes to the sink
there is the sound of water being run into the kettle*

There is the sound of the front door opening and closing

*Sarah comes into the living-room. She carries a full shopping basket and
a plastic carrier bag. She looks surprised to see Peter*

Sarah Oh, hello.
Peter Hello. I'm sorry to interrupt your Saturday.
Sarah You want to look round again?
Peter No. Just a couple of business matters to discuss with your husband.

Frank comes out of the kitchen

Frank Well, I would *rather* you did that through Mr Goodis.
Peter He wasn't in the office this morning, and I know you want to get
this through as quickly as possible, so . . .
Frank I've put the kettle on.
Sarah I'll make some tea. (*She takes her shopping out into the kitchen*)
Peter My surveyor's been very quick. He's a friend so he phoned me
about the survey. I took some notes. Of course he'll send me a typed-up
report next week, but I felt it only fair to tell you there are a few prob-
lems.
Frank Oh? What?
Peter Well, frankly it's a pretty bad report. I had noticed the cracks
myself—upstairs over the doors, and in here. But my surveyor noticed
big cracks in the brickwork outside.

*Sarah comes out of the kitchen, looking very worried. She has clearly
overheard*

Frank All old houses have cracks.
Peter Yes, but he says it's subsidence.
Sarah Subsidence?
Peter I'm afraid so. Extensive subsidence.

Sarah We've never had any trouble. There was nothing on our surveyor's report about subsidence.
Peter That *was* fourteen years ago, Mrs Gladwin.
Sarah I was here when your surveyor went round. He didn't say anything to me.
Peter He wouldn't, would he?

Sarah and Frank both look as though the roof has fallen in too

Frank So you're saying you don't want to go through with this?
Peter No. I didn't say that. I realized you'd be upset, so this morning I had my surveyor chat to a building contractor he knows—about what it would cost to put right. And I'd have it done after we've completed. *But* we would have to take the cost into consideration in the price.
Frank Oh? By how much?
Peter I thought ten thousand pounds would be fair. It's a big job—means propping up the foundations.

Sarah and Frank stare at him aghast. The kettle starts to whistle but Sarah doesn't seem to notice

Sarah You mean you want us to give you—ten thousand pounds?
Frank Sarah, the kettle.

She goes out to the kitchen, and turns the kettle off

Peter I'd have it done with the other structural changes. I'm going to be stuck with a huge bill, as it is. I'll have the whole conversion of the loft to do anyway.

Sarah comes out of the kitchen, but pointedly not bringing any tea

Frank What you're doing with the loft is no business of ours.
Sarah I'm surprised you're not putting a double-garage up there.

Peter feels their frost and tries a sympathetic smile

Peter Look, let's say eight thousand and I'll get this all through fast. I know you've exchanged contracts already.
Frank Oh, you do!
Peter I'll help you break out of this daisy chain, but you must help me too.
Frank By selling you our house at a knock-down price.
Peter Oh come on. Be realistic. Whoever you sell it to—any surveyor's going to . . .
Frank Any surveyor would put in a proper report—and not be a friend of yours.
Peter Are you suggesting . . .?
Frank Frankly, yes. You think you've got us over a barrel, because you've found out we've exchanged contracts.
Sarah I remember. I told you we were going to exchange on Friday, so you've waited till we've done it.
Peter Now, look here, if you think . . .

Frank I'd rather not sell this house at all than sell it to you. Go and tell someone else their house is falling down.

Peter (*getting up and giving them a cold smile*) Right. If that's the way you want it. Good luck.

Peter goes out. The front door bangs shut behind him

Sarah and Frank don't look at each other for a moment. He goes towards the drinks cupboard. She goes towards her desk

Frank (*turning back to her*) All right. Say it, and get it over with. I told you so. I told you that's what they were like. We should never have accepted their offer.

Sarah is still for an instant, then she lets go

Sarah Shit! Shit!

She picks up a manuscript and hurls it, so the pages scatter all over the floor.

Frank looks stunned

Shit!

Frank Come on. Don't talk like that.

Sarah Why not? Everybody else does. They say it on television. They write it on walls everywhere. *We're* so busy trying to be decent. What for? So some unscrupulous little bastard like him can try and rob us. Oh, what a bastard! What a shit!

Frank Sarah, stop it. You'd better take a Valium.

Sarah I don't want a bloody Valium. Why can't I have a nervous breakdown like everybody else? (*She sinks miserably on to the sofa*) We'll never sell this house. It's falling down.

Frank (*sitting next to her on the sofa*) Rubbish. He's probably trying it on.

Sarah But how do we know? Look at those cracks. Maybe he's right. Oh God, I don't care any more. I can't go on with this. I'm staying here. I'm not moving. (*She buries her head in her hands*)

CURTAIN

ACT II

When the CURTAIN *rises there is the sound of hammering, bricks being broken and chipped, ladders and furniture being moved and general builders' bustle. Over it is the sound of Jimmy whistling "Hello, Young Lovers", not quite as faithfully as Richard Rodgers might have liked. The whistling stops temporarily and breaks into "Getting To Know You"*

The Lights come up on the living-room. The door is open and wedged back, and there is a step-ladder open by the door-lintel, with a dust sheet covering the floor-area around the door. Jimmy Ryan is currently up the ladder whistling his snappy selection from "The King And I". He is a man of around thirty with a London accent that is not cockney. He is dealing with the cracks over the door. He has already filled them in and put lining paper over them and he is now painting over it, trying to match the colour to the rest of the wall. There is the sound of banging from the back of the house

Sarah comes out of the kitchen with a mug of tea

Sarah Tea, Jimmy.
Jimmy *(coming down the ladder)* Never say "no" to a cup of tea. Sugar in it? *(He takes the tea)*
Sarah Yes. Two, isn't it?
Jimmy That's right. Two for me. None for Kenneth, I'm the sweet one. You won't notice those cracks at all when I've finished.
Sarah *(not convinced)* No, the cracks are very good. The colour worries me a bit though.
Jimmy Ah, well, matching's a problem. It's bound to contrast a bit with the rest. Originally it was Antique White. Now I'd say it was more grubby than Antique. If you want no-one to notice I should really paint the whole room.
Sarah But we have to do this in four rooms. If we have to repaint them all—we just don't have the time.
Jimmy Well, if I'm to do a proper job . . .

The phone rings and Sarah answers it

Sarah Hello . . . Oh, Mr Goodis . . . No. I didn't say we were taking it off the market. Just that we don't want anyone viewing it this week . . . We're—er—having a pipe repaired . . . Had a small leak . . . Why? Have you got someone who's interested? You've heard nothing from the Fearnleys? No, well if anyone is interested they can come next week. Yes, I know we're cutting it fine. Bye. *(She puts the phone down)*
Jimmy Very wise not to let the word get out about the subsidence.

Sarah I told you. It's not subsidence. It's settlement. We had a surveyor in, and he said it was absolutely normal for an old house.

Jimmy Right. And with the cracks repaired no-one will notice anything. Mind you, those surveyors never agree about anything. People just use them to bring the price down.

Sarah Exactly. Now, about matching this paint.

Jimmy Never match it properly.

Sarah But your firm said you could. Can't you tone it down somehow—dirty it?

Jimmy Dirty it?

Sarah Yes. So it doesn't stand out like a sore thumb.

Jimmy looks round the room thoughtfully and notices the fireplace

Jimmy You light a fire in there ever?

Sarah Last Christmas we had one. Smokeless fuel.

Jimmy Soot. Might be some soot up there. That could work. Secret with soot is in the mixing. You've got to mix it properly.

He drains his mug of tea, and gets the mixing stick from his pot of brushes. He takes the empty mug and stick and goes over to the fireplace. Sarah watches him curiously. He reaches up and scrapes around inside the chimney, holding the empty mug to catch the soot

We're in luck. You've got soot. I knew someone who used soot once. For a job just like this one. But he didn't mix it properly, when he'd finished the wall looked like a zebra crossing.

Sarah Do you think it will work?

Jimmy (*taking a mugful of soot over to his paint-pot*) Can but try, as Van Gogh said. (*He picks up the pot of paint and brush*) I'll experiment outside—just in case it doesn't.

Sarah I'll be working in here if you want me.

Jimmy exits through the kitchen

Sarah goes to her desk, sits down and starts to look at a manuscript

Liz comes down the stairs and into the room. She is dressed in "going-to-first-rehearsal" clothes and carries a script

Liz Morning.

Sarah Good morning.

Liz Any coffee on?

Sarah No. Tea. I've made two lots already. They don't drink coffee. I think it keeps them awake.

Liz What were they doing outside?

Sarah Pointing.

Liz I saw my painters yesterday. They'll only be another couple of days.

Sarah Oh good. I'm glad you'd rather live with my painters than yours.

Liz Didn't sleep well, did you?

Sarah No. What time is your rehearsal?

Liz Twelve. No-one should be asked to play a drunken shoplifter before lunch.

Sarah I'm sure you'll manage. (*She checks herself*) The tea will still be hot. Why don't you have some?

Liz puts her script on the sofa and goes out to the kitchen to get some tea. Sarah tries to concentrate on making some notes about the manuscript in front of her but can hear Liz saying her lines

Liz "I paid for the two bras and nightie, didn't I? . . . the two bras and nightie, didn't I? I picked up the pants afterwards." (*She comes out of the kitchen with a cup of tea, goes and sits on the sofa and starts looking at her script*)

Sarah tries to go on concentrating on her reading but becomes aware of Liz saying the lines under her breath, inflecting them differently

(*Sotto voce*) "I paid for the two bras and nightie, didn't I? . . . the two bras and nightie, didn't I? I picked up the pants afterwards."

Sarah is clearly being aggravated by the stage-whisper

"I picked up the tights afterwards. I had a lot on my mind."

Sarah can't stand it any longer. She gathers up her manuscript, stands up and starts to go towards the door

(*To Sarah*) Sorry, am I disturbing you?
Sarah (*grimly*) No. No. That's all right. You're going to be on television. (*Waving the manuscript at her*) This is probably never going to be published.

Sarah exits up the stairs

Liz stares after her, shrugs and goes back to her script. She abandons the sotto voce and tries it properly with a slightly tipsy voice

Liz "I paid for the two bras and nightie, didn't I?"

Jimmy comes into the kitchen with his pot of paint and appears in the archway. He stares at Liz, imagining her to be in conversation with someone else in the room

(*Without noticing Jimmy*) "I picked up the pants afterwards. I had a lot on my mind. My kid's on probation, my husband's behind with his alimony payments. All right there *were* six pairs of pants. Christ, you're carrying on like I was going to bankrupt Marks and Spencers."

Jimmy starts to whistle discreetly and comes into the room. Liz swings round. Jimmy looks to see if anyone else is there and then looks at her as though she might be a little touched

Jimmy All right if I—er—get on with the painting?
Liz Yes, fine. I was just trying to learn my lines.

Jimmy Ah! For a moment there I thought you were having a row with Mrs Gladwin.

Liz I don't normally steal her underwear.

Jimmy (*going up the ladder with his pot and brush*) Been dirtying the paint. I get some funny jobs these days.

Jimmy starts whistling "My Favourite Things" from "The Sound of Music". At first he whistles softly, but, as he paints, it gets louder. Liz goes back to saying her lines to herself, trying to learn them and throwing in a few gestures

Liz (*acting both parts*) "But you'd been drinking before?" "Yes, your honour. I'd had a few drinks." "Where?" "In the pub. I'd met a friend. I was just walking down the road, minding my own business when I met this fellow I hadn't seen for ages . . ."

Liz finds Jimmy's whistling distracting. She tries but cannot concentrate, especially as he hasn't got the tune quite right. Exasperated, she gives up, picks up her script and heads for the door

I'll do this upstairs. Don't want to disturb you.

Liz moves round the ladder and goes out up the stairs

Jimmy frowns, puzzling over her exit line. He shrugs. The phone rings and he comes down the ladder and answers it

Jimmy Hello, this is Jimmy . . . No chance Roger, I'm going to be here the rest of the week. You shouldn't have told them we could match up this paint. I've tried everything . . . I've even mucked up Antique White with soot, and it still looks bloody terrible . . . Yes. I suppose some grey might help. What about some of that Medieval Grey? . . . O.K. You need to be bleedin' Michael Angelo to work in this place. (*He puts the phone down and massages his neck and shoulders, as though trying to relax his muscles. He goes back up the ladder and starts painting again*)

There is the sound of the front door opening and closing

Jane Gladwin comes in. She is about nineteen, and is dressed in fashionably sloppy student clothes: jeans, tee-shirt, and a hard-used anorak. She carries a duffel-bag, and looks washed-out. She stares up in surprise at Jimmy on the ladder

Jane Hello.

Jimmy (*sitting up, looking embarrassed*) Hello. (*He picks up the book, scrambles up and puts it back on the shelf*)

Jane You're redecorating the place? I thought they were selling it. I'm Jane, their daughter.

Jimmy Ah. They're selling it all right but they've got a bit of a problem. Some chap told them the house is falling down.

Jane It's not, is it?

Jimmy No. When did you last see a house fall down?

Jane (*throwing her duffel-bag on an armchair*) I'm going to make some tea. You want a cup?

Jimmy Never say "no" to a cup of tea.

Janes goes into the kitchen

    Sarah comes down the stairs and into the room. She spots and recognizes the duffel-bag on the chair

Sarah Whose is that?

Jimmy Your daughter's.

Jane appears in the doorway

Jane Hello, Mum.

Sarah Jane. What are you doing here? I thought . . . Are you all right?

Jane Why shouldn't I be all right?

Sarah It's term still. And you don't look—very well.

Jane I've just put the kettle on.

Jimmy is tactful enough to realize his presence is not welcome. He comes down the ladder

Jimmy I'll go and see how Kenneth's getting on with the pointing.

Jane takes off her anorak and slings it over the other armchair, both she and Sarah waiting until Jimmy leaves

    He exits through the kitchen

Sarah All right. What's gone wrong at college?

Jane Nothing. Except I've left.

Sarah What do you mean . . .? Why?

Jane Because I've spent this term's allowance.

Sarah You can't have. What on?

Jane An abortion.

Sarah is stunned. She sits down suddenly on the arm of the armchair

Sarah Oh no. No. Why . . .

Jane Because I didn't want a baby. Why else?

Sarah I meant why couldn't you have told us first?

Jane It seemed like my business. (*Her attitude towards her mother is aggressive, as though attack is the best form of defence*)

Sarah When? When was . . .

Jane Yesterday. They kept me in for twenty-four hours.

The kettle is heard whistling

    Jimmy enters through the back door and quickly turns the kettle off. He makes the tea in the background

Sarah and Jane don't seem to notice that the kettle has been turned off

Sarah Are you—all right?

Jane Oh, don't worry. It wasn't a back-street job. For a term's allowance you can afford St John's Wood. All very hygienic. Most of the girls in there were foreign. Apparently it's still cheaper here.

Jimmy comes out of the kitchen carrying a tray with two mugs of tea on it and a sugar-bowl. Sarah spots him just in time to sound more casual

Sarah Thank God something is.

Jimmy I've made some more tea, if you'd like some.

Sarah Thank you, Jimmy.

Jimmy (*putting the tray down on the coffee-table*) I'll take some out to Kenneth.

Sarah Thank you, Jimmy.

Jimmy Pointing's going nicely outside. Never spot any sub—er—settlement now.

Sarah Thank you, Jimmy.

Jimmy exits through the kitchen

Why couldn't you have told us?

Jane Why? So Dad could have got it for me on the National Health?

Sarah No. I thought you'd have . . . I thought we could at least have discussed . . .

Jane Wasn't much to discuss. I was careless.

Sarah But whoever was responsible . . .

Jane I was responsible.

Sarah Oh, come on. It wasn't an immaculate conception.

Jane His name was Simon. He was third year.

Sarah What did he think about it?

Jane I didn't tell him. I discovered I didn't like him enough.

Sarah A bit late, wasn't it?

Jane They told me to rest for a couple of days.

Sarah I'll get Dr Green to come over . . .

Jane No, thanks. I don't want anybody else prodding me around. I'll go up and lie down. That chap says the house is falling down.

Sarah Well, it isn't.

Jane exits up the stairs

Sarah stares after her and then sits down, still stunned

Jimmy enters the kitchen whistling. He comes to the archway and looks sympathetically at Sarah, clearly knowing what is going on

Jimmy I'll clear away some of this stuff now if that's all right.

Sarah Yes. Of course.

The phone rings but Sarah doesn't move. Finally, Jimmy answers it

Jimmy Hello . . . I'll go and see if she's in. Who's speaking? . . . (*Covering the mouthpiece, to Sarah*) It's Susan. From the office. Shall I tell them you'll call back?

Sarah No. I'll take it. (*She gets up and goes to the phone*)

Jimmy goes back to his paint-pot and goes up the ladder, eager not to miss anything without looking obvious about it

Hello, Susan . . . I know, I'm sorry. I've just done those reports. You'll have them tomorrow . . . What pages? . . . *Away Game* . . . Oh Lord, the Newcastle dwarf. They got muddled up with some of my husband's papers. He said he'd find them. I keep forgetting to remind him . . . Yes. I will. I—I—(*her voice breaks, near to tears*)—I'll call you to-morrow, Susan. (*She puts the phone down and sits stock still*)

Jimmy, whistling "Getting To Know You", takes the step-ladder and paint-pots and exits through the kitchen

Black-out

Sarah takes the tray and goes into the kitchen as Jimmy's whistling is heard loudly on the tape

The Lights come up

The dust sheet has been removed. The area above the door seems to be finished, but there are visibly different squares of colour; old and new

Frank comes in from work, carrying an evening paper. He looks up and inspects the paintwork over the door

Sarah comes in from the kitchen. She looks apprehensive

Frank Hello.
Sarah Hello.
Frank I see he's had a go up there. I suppose it will look all right when it's finished.
Sarah Yes.
Frank Don't want any more Bellings trying to force the price down. (*He puts the evening paper on the dining-table*)
Sarah No. I just wish he would stop talking as though he's some art-restorer tarting-up a fake.
Frank Did you tell him our surveyor says it's just normal settlement?
Sarah Yes.
Frank Is he still whistling?
Sarah When he's not drinking tea. It's driving me mad.
Frank Any word from Goodis?
Sarah He phoned.
Frank And?
Sarah The idiot got a message we'd taken the house off the market.
Frank Oh no.
Sarah I told him it was only while we had a pipe repaired.
Frank Had he heard from the Fearnleys?
Sarah No.
Frank I told you that woman was potty. After the renovations we'll be starting the merry-go-round again from scratch. With completion on the flat in five weeks.
Sarah I know.

Frank I'd better go and change. This damn dinner's at eight.
Sarah Did you write your speech?
Frank Yes. Is Liz in?
Sarah No. She's out for the evening.
Frank I'll take a drink up and get ready. Do you want one? (*He pours himself a Scotch*)
Sarah No. You'd better make it a strong one.
Frank It's only a six-line speech. Two dental jokes and the word welcome in four languages.
Sarah I didn't mean that.
Frank Oh? What then?
Sarah Jane's here.
Frank Now? Why isn't she at college? Is she sick? Oh Lord, she's pregnant?
Sarah No, worse. Or better, I don't know. She's just had an abortion.

Frank freezes, staring at Sarah

Yesterday. She used her term's allowance. Says she's not going back to college.
Frank Oh—no. Couldn't she have told us she was in trouble? We've always . . . I thought we'd . . .
Sarah Apparently she thinks it's no longer any of our business.
Frank The bloody stupid . . . poor girl. Is she all right?
Sarah She says so. She's been in her room all afternoon playing records —and typing.
Frank I'll go up and see her.
Sarah I don't think that's a good idea—at the moment.
Frank I don't understand. I mean—doesn't she take precautions?
Sarah Not this time apparently.
Frank Did she tell you who's responsible?
Sarah She says she is.
Frank Oh, very liberated! Well, whoever he was, he didn't have to have an abortion.
Sarah His name's Simon. He's a student, and she doesn't seem to care for him anymore.
Frank Simon who?
Sarah Does it matter?
Frank Do the college know?
Sarah She didn't tell them. Just walked out.
Frank She's got to go back.
Sarah Says she won't.
Frank Rubbish. What's she going to do?
Sarah Says she's going to get a job.
Frank Oh, yes. Her and the other two and a half million. What's she going to get after a year at college and a successful abortion?
Sarah She says she knows someone on some new magazine who might give her some work.
Frank What magazine?

Sarah It sounds to me like a consumer guide to teenage sex.

Frank Bloody stupid girl. She wants to ruin her whole life because she forgot to take a pill. What's she trying to prove—that she can get herself pregnant? (*He goes and slumps miserably in an armchair with his drink*)

Sarah Calm down. You're going to give yourself a heart attack.

Frank I won't have given it to myself—not in this house.

Sarah I spoke to Dr Green. He says she's bound to be depressed for a few days.

Frank What about us?

Sarah Come on. You should go and change. You'll be late.

Frank I'm not going *now*.

Sarah You won't do any good hanging around here. You just come home as soon as you can.

Frank (*nodding and getting up*) I suppose so. I'll try and talk to her.

Sarah All right, but don't go on at her about it.

Frank I won't even mention it. I'll ask her about her teeth

He goes out

Black-out. In the darkness a Joni Mitchell record, "Jericho", comes up softly. Over it is the sound of a knocking on a door

Frank's voice Jane . . . Jane. Come on, Jane. I've got to go out. I want to talk to you. Do you hear me? Open the door. Jane, don't be stupid.

The music is turned up. There is a furious knocking over the music, which reaches a crescendo, and then dies down

The Lights come up

The lamps are turned on and there is some cold supper left on the table and a place set for one. Sarah sits in an armchair reading a manuscript and making notes

Jane comes in wearing an old dressing-gown

Sarah looks up at her and smiles as warmly as she can manage

Sarah How do you feel?

Jane Not marvellous.

Sarah I've left you some quiche and salad, if you feel like it. I've eaten. I was starving.

Jane goes over and inspects the food without enthusiasm. She gets a piece of quiche, sits down and disconsolately chews a mouthful. In the silence, Sarah glances at her

There's some white wine Liz left in the fridge. She's been staying a few days. She's been rehearsing for a new television, a courtroom drama. She's playing a drunken shoplifter.

Jane goes out to the kitchen. Sarah glances at her manuscript, trying to appear casual as Jane comes back to the table with a half-full bottle of

wine and a glass. Jane fills her glass, leaving the bottle on the table and then drinks and eats as she wanders round the room

Dad's gone to a dinner. Common Market Dentists. He had to make a speech.

Jane sits down, chewing and drinking. Sarah is clearly irritated by her manners but tries not to show it

He'll use his two old dental jokes and his motto for Periodontists . . .
Jane Oh, for Christ's sakes, Mum.
Sarah What's wrong?
Jane You're behaving as though there's an unexploded bomb in the room.
Sarah I thought you'd been detonated.

Stung, Jane goes sullen

Jane That's typical.
Sarah Typical of what?
Jane Of you. Always having the right *word*. You're so proud of that. Command of language. Keeping your Oxford English degree alive. Your middle-class concern with—
Sarah Oh, no. Not that again.

Jane gets up angrily, crosses to the table and refills her glass

Jane You've always got just the right *word*, haven't you? I don't think any of us ever won an argument with you. Poor Ben least of all.
Sarah I suppose it would show too much middle-class concern if you asked if *I* wanted a glass of wine.
Jane Would you like a glass of wine?
Sarah No, thank you, I think I'll have something stronger. (*She goes to the upper drinks cupboard. She opens it, rummages around and pulls out a bottle of Green Chartreuse*) I suppose someone has to drink some of these at some point. (*She pours some of the sticky green stuff into a liquuer glass*)
Jane (*leaving her glass on the dining-table and wandering over to the desk*) And you always had the *last* word too. That's why Ben left you a note when he went to America.

Sarah leaves the bottle on top of the cupboard and crosses to an armchair. Jane sits at the desk, and registers Sarah's tape-recorder and presses the playback-button

Sarah's voice (*on tape*) When you take away the throbbing, vibrant clichés, and separate the firm breasts from the soft buttocks you haven't a lot left.
Jane (*stopping the tape*) Now the words you save on us you use on those poor manuscripts. The best lit. crit. That's what I've been studying for a year. Analysing and criticizing other people's writing. Polishing my little essays every week, having them criticized. Why? So I can end up like you.

Sarah Oh that's nonsense. We always tried to treat you both as indivi-
duals . . .

Jane (*getting up and pacing*) Who had to fit in with your attitudes. You've
always taken attitudes to everything. You've taken one to this *situation*.
Talked *sensibly* to Dad about it. Let's be *reasonable*. Not raise our
voices.

Sarah What should I do? Apologize that I'm not Italian? Is being
reasonable so terrible?

Jane It's not reasonable, it's patronizing. It's the assumption you know
it all. That we'll end up like you. Right, left, bent or straight, it's all a
phase. You've read about it—and *understand*. So you can smile indul-
gently, and wait for it to pass.

Sarah And that's really how we seem to you? Dull and smug.

Jane No—not all the time—but, Christ, this past year, whenever I've
been at home, all you two seem to care about is buying and selling
houses. I watched you both one night—watching the telly news. The
first item was a war somewhere, the second was a famine somewhere
else—and then there was something about the mortgage rates. That's
what turned you on—some dry old bugger droning on about a half per
cent reduction. Dad said that would really move the market.

Sarah (*getting up and putting her glass on the dining-table*) It didn't. I'd
have thought this situation with the house would appeal to you. It's
quite symbolic, isn't it? I mean here we are, the beleaguered bour-
geoisie—our foundations suspect—papering over the cracks in order to
abandon the place, and get into something smaller. Come on, you
ought to go to bed. Your father's late. I'm not waiting up for him. (*She
switches off the standard lamp*)

Jane I don't want one of his lectures in the morning.

Sarah (*switching off wall-bracket lights*) He doesn't talk much these
mornings. The builders come early. They may need to do your room
tomorrow too.

Jane Even when I'm sick, selling this bloody house comes first for you,
doesn't it?

Sarah (*putting her arm round Jane*) You've solved your problem. I'm
still trying to solve mine. You need a good night's sleep.

Jane I haven't slept properly for weeks. Oh God, I feel terrible.

Sarah Hang on. (*She goes to her desk, gets the bottle of Valium, takes a
tablet out and replaces the bottle, and then comes back and gives it to
Jane*) Have one of these. It'll help.

Jane What is it?

Sarah A tranquillizer.

Jane Since when have you been taking tranquillizers?

Sarah Only since we got involved in this moving business. Soon they'll
be letting estate-agents write the prescriptions. (*She switches off the
lamp* UR)

Black-out

Sarah and Jane go out, closing the door behind them

There is a pause for a few moments

> *The door opens and Frank comes in, lit by the light in the hall. He switches on the lamp* UR *and then the standard lamp. He wears a dinner-jacket and looks slightly the worse for wear. He goes to the record-stack, selects a record and puts it on. It is Vivaldi's "Concerto for Guitar and Strings in, D Major". It comes up very loud and, startled, he turns it down. He spots the Green Chartreuse bottle on top of the drinks cupboard. Puzzled, he picks it up and looks at it. He is going to put it away, and then decides on a nightcap. He pours a fair quantity into a sherry-glass and tries it. It clearly warms him. He goes and sits in an armchair, beating time to the music, humming falsetto to it. He stretches his legs, puts his head back*

There is the sound of the front-door opening and closing

> *Liz comes into the living-room. She wears her short, fur jacket over a dress and has clearly had a heavy night out too*

Frank sits up, surprised to see her

Liz Oh, it's you.
Frank Oh, hello, Liz.
Liz Oh, come on. Isn't that a bit chi-chi? Putting on a dinner jacket to listen to Vivaldi, *and* drinking Creme de Menthe?
Frank I've been to a dinner. It's Green Chartreuse anyway.
Liz Even more chic.
Frank Do you want some?
Liz No. It's too good to go on top of what I've been drinking. Oh, all right. (*She goes and pours herself some into a sherry-glass*)
Frank Have you had a good evening?
Liz No. Rotten food and shop-talk.
Frank Me too.
Liz Cheers.
Frank Cheers.

They drink

Liz (*grimacing*) Christ, this is strong.
Frank I found it left out. Sarah must have had some.
Liz Sarah? To cope with Jane, I suppose.
Frank You know about that?
Liz Yes. I'm sorry.
Frank I wish I could understand why she . . . (*He goes to the hi-fi and switches off the record*)
Liz You're probably not meant to. Leave it on if you like.
Frank No. It's a night for Wagner anyway.

She pats him commiseratingly on the shoulder

We always thought that if she was—going to do that sort of thing .
Liz Frank, why can't you say "screw around"?
Frank Must I?
Liz You'd seem more human to her. To your patients too.
Frank My patients?

Liz Yes, you'd be a fun dentist. (*Wagging a finger at an imaginary patient*) If you go on screwing around like that all your teeth will go rotten.

Frank You're a silly bitch, Liz.

Liz I'm trying to cheer you up. (*She sits cross-legged on the floor, resting her back against the sofa*)

Frank Thanks. I was a real fun dentist tonight. Made a speech. Told a joke.

Liz Did they laugh?

Frank I was too bloody miserable to notice.

Liz What was the joke?

Frank drinks

Frank Motto for periodontists. If you can keep your teeth while all around you are losing theirs.

Liz All your own? Not bad for a dentist.

Frank You've really got it in for the professional classes, haven't you? All the popular prejudices. Lawyers—dry. Doctors—dull. Dentists— boring. It all comes from bad TV.

Liz Or having been married to a doctor.

Frank John just happened to be a doctor. He'd have been a stupid sod whatever he did.

Liz I thought you liked him.

Frank No. Always thought you were wasted on him.

Liz Oh, Frank. That's nice. The green stuff agrees with you. I think maybe dentists are nicer than doctors.

Frank (*getting up and getting the bottle of Green Chartreuse*) Well, most people prefer doctors. At least they lay you out before they hurt you.

Liz Why did you become a dentist?

Frank My practical streak, I suppose. Most ordinary doctors just sit there and listen to your pains and woes. If there's anything really wrong with you it's off to a hospital or a psychiatrist. Dentists actually fix you up all by themselves. If we get it wrong you don't actually die.

Liz You just spit all your teeth out.

Frank And we give you shiny new ones that look better than the old, clapped-out, yellow ones. (*He sits on the sofa and puts the bottle on the coffee-table*)

Liz You're really a happy dentist, aren't you?

Frank I was—till Sarah decided our lives needed change.

Liz Hers. Not yours.

Frank Yes. I suppose so. Oh God, I don't understand her.

Liz Sarah?

Frank No. Jane. I can't understand why she got into this mess.

Liz She must have wanted it that way. I mean these days you've really got to work at it to get pregnant. Do you know I didn't switch to the pill till I was thirty.

Frank In my day, they were still trying it out on mice. I remember sidling into chemists' shops, praying there wasn't a girl behind the counter, or I'd have to ask for aspirins.

Sarah comes in, without their noticing, and goes to the kitchen, switching on the light

Liz Ah, French letters! Where are they now?

Frank In bloody slot-machines in every loo. First one of those I saw I thought it was a new-fangled soap-dispenser.

They laugh and drink, Sarah is starting to mix a bicarbonate of soda. The sound of the spoon in the glass makes them swing round

Sarah (*from the kitchen*) Don't let me disturb you. I'm just getting some bicarbonate of soda.

Frank and Liz suddenly look very self-conscious. Liz gets up from the floor and gathers up her things

Liz I think I'm going to turn in. (*She puts her glass on the coffee-table*)

Frank (*in a loud whisper*) Why does she want bicarbonate of soda?

Sarah appears from the kitchen. In one hand she has a glassful of water bubbling with bicarbonate of soda, with a spoon in it

Sarah Because we've run out of Alka-Seltzer. (*Indicating the Green Chartreuse*) I had some of that. It's given me appalling heartburn. It seems to be agreeing with both of you.

There is an uneasy silence, Frank sinks into the sofa. Sarah drinks some bicarb, pulls a face, and suppresses an instant belch. Liz looks from one to the other

Liz I'm going to bed. Night all.

She goes out, closing the door behind her

Sarah I'm sorry I broke up the party. I thought you were still out boozing with the international gum-brigade.

Frank rests his head on his hands, gloom redescending

Frank I did that too.

Sarah You've had quite a night then.

Frank You told me I'd be no use round here this evening.

Sarah That was yesterday evening. It's two-thirty now. I had an earful of Jane, and then I couldn't sleep. (*She starts to clear the dining-table, taking things out to the kitchen*)

Frank Jane actually said something?

Sarah Yes. One of her social protest speeches—about me.

Frank We've got to persuade her to go back to college, one drop-out in the family is enough.

Sarah (*switching off the light and coming out of the kitchen*) I'd like to drop out right now. Oh God, what a day!

Frank Yes, me too. I made a nice mess of someone's jaw this afternoon. Had to put in six extra stitches.

He reaches out, almost instinctively, for the bottle. She stops his hand and puts her half-drunk glass of bicarb in it

What's this?

Sarah You're always telling me prevention is better than cure.

He drinks a mouthful and pulls a face. She puts another teaspoonful in and it fizzes

Drink it down in one.

He does, and belches. She sits down on the sofa and puts the bicarb tin down on the coffee-table, next to the Chartreuse

Frank Oh, I've had it, Sarah.

Sarah Had what?

Frank This whole nonsense. Jane, Ben, the house, builders, buyers. Surveyors, solicitors, contracts, completion. I don't want that flat anymore. We can't go through with it. It won't be big enough anyway, will it? When Auntie Sophie breaks down, we'll get your mother. Jane needs a bedroom to lock herself in. Ben's bound to come back and need a room for a chapel. Full house.

Sarah We've signed the contract, we'd lose our seven thousand pounds deposit. That's what you said when *I* changed my mind.

Frank That was *you* deciding to lose my money. I feel better when it's my decision.

Sarah *Your* money?

Frank Yes. I happen to have earned most of it.

Sarah Oh God. I never thought *you'd* say that.

Frank Oh, I know, if you hadn't got married, had our children, run our house you'd have been Jonathan Cape—or Chief Penguin at Penguin Books. All right—*hypothetically* some of it's your money, but, damn it, we'll lose that in six months' interest if we don't sell this.

Sarah We're going to move—preferably when you're sober.

Frank Fine bloody family we are. Our son reborn, our daughter—the opposite.

Sarah Don't leave me out. I'm sure you can find something wrong with me.

Frank Yes, if you insist. For the past year you've been a glorified estate-agent—when you've not got your nose in a rotten book that isn't going to be published anyway.

Sarah You resent me doing anything except being here to have your dinner ready at seven and turn the electric blanket on at eleven.

Frank Oh Christ, when have we ever got to bed at eleven?

Sarah Because you sit here like a zombie playing your bloody baroque music all night.

Frank Why not? Haven't we had enough of Mammon all day? Buying, selling, how much we'll make, or lose. What furniture we'll have to replace. Damn it, I've had it.

Sarah So what are you going to do? Walk out on us?

Frank Walk out? Where to? I can't afford to walk out. The only place I could afford to stay is my dentist's chair at the hospital.

Sarah You'd be very comfy. It reclines to one-hundred-and-eighty degrees. I wish to hell you would. You're no damn use round here.

Frank moves, a little unsteadily for full dignity, towards the door

Frank I'll sleep in the spare room. There is one left, isn't there?

Sarah If not, you can always share with Liz. I'm sure she won't mind.

Frank If I'm going to—to screw around—it won't be with your sister.

Frank storms out, banging the door

Black-out

   During the following taped dialogue Sarah exits and changes and then, she, Frank and Liz enter and sit at the dining-table

There is a hammering and then the sound of knocking on a door

Frank's voice (*pained*) Yes?

Sarah's voice How long are you going to be in the bathroom?

Frank's voice All day. I've been sick. (*He groans*)

The banging starts up again

   Can you hear that too?

Sarah's voice Of course I can hear it.

Frank's voice Thank God.

Sarah's voice It's the builders. They're finishing off the back.

Frank's voice Send them away. We don't need them. We're staying here.

The banging becomes intermittent

The Lights come up and the hammering continues

Frank and Sarah are having breakfast at opposite ends of the table. Liz sits between them. The normal breakfast things are on the table, and a folded copy of "The Guardian". On an armchair are Frank's jacket and briefcase. Sarah eats her toast, set-faced, clearly not talking to Frank, who looks in a very delicate condition. Liz looks from one to the other in the silence. She seems to have survived the night better than the other two, and is quietly amused by the situation. The hammering stops

Liz Well, the hammering has stopped.

There is a silence. Then Jimmy's whistling starts up off stage and they react

   Aren't you going to ask me to ask Frank to pass you the marmalade?

Sarah I don't take marmalade.

Liz Ah! Want the salt, Frank?

Frank I don't take it in my coffee.

There is another silence. In the frost, Liz acts with forced cheerfulness

Liz Maybe you shouldn't move after all.

Frank We're not.

Sarah He's not.
Liz But you are?
Sarah Yes.
Liz Won't it be different just to sell half a house?

There is a noise from the hall of letters coming through the door

That sounds like letters. I'll get them.

Liz goes out

Sarah looks coldly at Frank

Sarah (*picking up the coffee-pot*) Do you want some more coffee?
Frank No. It will make me feel sick again.
Sarah I envy your lucky patients this morning. By the way, did your secretary find those pages from that manuscript?
Frank Oh, sorry I forgot . . .

Liz comes back with the letters

Liz Mostly for you, Frank. Looks like bills.

She hands them to Frank who glances at them and chucks them down on the table

There's a letter from Ben. (*She holds up an airmail letter*)
Sarah A letter? (*She takes it*)
Frank He's actually written.
Sarah Maybe he's lost his voice.
Liz Has he still got his head shaved?
Frank No. Buddhism was last year's religion. He sent us a photo. He's got long hair and a beard now. He's twenty-one and he looks like Tolstoy at eighty-two. (*To Sarah*) Is he still going to be born again?
Sarah Next month.
Liz Does that mean you won't be his parents anymore?
Sarah He doesn't say. He's hoping to come home at Christmas and stay a while. The Reverend Hoskins says there's a lot of work to be done in Britain. He's thinking of starting a mission here.
Frank Oh good. That's just what Britain needs—more religious maniacs.
Sarah He blesses us all. (*She bows her head*) Well, at least, we'll have them both home for Christmas.
Frank You told me our kids had left home. That's why we were moving.

Jane comes in, and goes silently to the table

Welcome home.

Jane nods

Good-morning.
Jane Hi.
Sarah (*to Jane*) Do you want some cereal?
Frank (*to Liz*) We don't say good-morning round here anymore. It's not fashionable to say good-morning. It's too much effort. It's got three syllables.

Jane stiffens, gets up and goes to the door

Jane Bad-tempered old bugger. (*After a pause*) That's got six syllables.

Jane goes out

Sarah I told you not to say anything.
Frank What are we supposed to do? Not open our mouths till she gets pregnant again?
Sarah Why don't you just go to work?
Frank I'm going. Goodbye. (*He gets his briefcase*)
Liz Frank. If you can keep your teeth while all around you . . .

Frank goes out

Sarah (*staring suspiciously at Liz*) How do *you* know that?
Liz Frank and I meet furtively at periodontal dinners. He told me last night. You're getting paranoid, Sarah.
Sarah Why not? I might as well be as screwed up as the rest of this family. Ben's barmy, Jane's a mess, Frank's drinking.
Liz Drinking. You're neurotic about people drinking. I have a few drinks and you start behaving as if I'm an alcoholic. Anything that seems at all out-of-control really menaces you, doesn't it?
Sarah I wish you'd stop sounding like one of your analysts.
Liz I'm sorry.

Jimmy starts to whistle, off

Anyway, after rehearsal today, I'm going back to my place.
Sarah There's no need.

The sound of Jimmy whistling the introduction to "Oh, What A Beautiful Morning" wafts in from the kitchen and then Jimmy goes to the sink and the sound of a running tap is heard

Oh God, there's a bright golden haze on the meadow.
Liz Have you noticed—he only does Rodgers and Hammerstein?
Sarah Yes, he does.

Jimmy comes in with a pot of paint and brushes

Jimmy Good-morning.
Liz Good-morning.
Jimmy All right if I start on the cracks in the bedroom now?
Sarah Yes.

Liz clears the breakfast things, leaving the cornflakes, milk, and one place setting, and takes them out into the kitchen

Jimmy (*looking at the wall*) A touch of that Medieval Grey helped, didn't it?
Sarah Yes. Will you be able to match it any better in the bedrooms?
Jimmy Should be easier with mushroom. It's a dirtier colour to start with.
Sarah Is all the pointing finished?

Jimmy Very nearly. Kenneth's gone off to another job today. So it's only one for tea this morning.
Sarah I'll make some.

He goes out through the door whistling "I Cain't Say No" from "Oklahoma"

Sarah turns to go into the kitchen and Liz comes out

Liz It's O.K. The kettle's on.
Sarah Look, if you're going down to see Mum on Saturday why don't you stay here till then?
Liz I've scrounged enough already. And now you've got Jane here . . .
Sarah I'd like you to stay.
Liz O.K.

The kettle starts to whistle

At least *that* doesn't do *Oklahoma*. I'll make the tea. (*She goes back to the kitchen*)

Sarah goes over to her desk. She opens a drawer and gets out a bottle of Valium. She takes one and comes back to swallow it with the remains of Liz's cold coffee

(*Coming out of the kitchen*) I've made the tea. Do I take it to him?
Sarah No, he comes. He's got a very good nose for tea. He can smell it at a hundred yards. (*She pauses*)

There is the sound of Jimmy coming back, whistling. The whistling comes closer and then Jimmy comes in

Jimmy Sorry to bother you, but can't get into the back bedroom. Door's locked.
Sarah Oh, that's my daughter.
Jimmy Didn't like to disturb her. She—er—feeling better today?
Sarah Yes, thanks. I'll go and tell her you want to do the room.
Liz I'm going up. I'll tell her.
Sarah Thanks.

Liz goes out

(*To Jimmy*) There's tea made. I'll get you some.
Jimmy No, no. You carry on with what you're doing. I'll get it.

Jimmy goes into the kitchen. Sarah goes to her desk to get out a manuscript. The whistling starts up again from the kitchen. Sarah winces at the sound of it. She shuts her eyes, puts her hands to the back of her neck and tries to relax it. Jimmy comes out of the kitchen with his mug of tea

You all right?
Sarah Yes. Just a slight pain in the neck.
Jimmy Ah! I know just the thing for that. That's tension. Everybody has it these days. You probably get it a lot, sitting tensely, poring over those manuscripts.

Sarah Yes.

Jimmy I get it. Especially painting. All round here—the neck—and shoulders. So when I feel tense now I stop, and do the Alexander Method.

Sarah What is that?

Jimmy Well, the basic theory is our vertebrae are this thin, delicate column, but they have to support this big, heavy skull. Most of us don't carry ourselves properly, so when we tense up we take all the strain here—and here—and you develop a hump. This is what you do. You get a book. (*He goes to bookcase and selects a thick book and then glances at the title*) *War and Peace*. That always does the trick. The book needs to be about three inches thick. (*He puts the book on the floor, lies down on his back, resting his head on the book*) You rest your head on it. Then you talk to your muscles and order them to relax. You order your neck to go free, your head to go forward and upwards, your back to lengthen and widen. Then your knees come up and away. Now if you feel my hump . . .

Sarah Where is it?

He takes her hand and puts it on the back of his neck

Jimmy See, it's disappeared.

Liz comes in

Liz Sarah, I'm just off—(*seeing Jimmy stretched out and Sarah bending over him she rushes up to bend over them*)—Christ, what's happened?

Sarah His skull is too heavy for his vertebrae.

Jimmy The Alexander Method. Very good for the back. (*He gets up*)

Liz Ah well, I'm off to rehearsals. Jane's coming down. Bye.

Liz straightens up and goes out

Jimmy I'll give you a proper lesson sometime.

Sarah Oh thank you, Jimmy.

Jimmy Right then, I'll go up and start rendering the wall.

Jimmy goes to the door whistling as Jane comes in

Jane Morning.

Jimmy Hello.

Jimmy exits upstairs

Jane (*going and sitting down to her breakfast*) That man is either hammering or whistling.

Sarah It must be a lot quieter at college.

Jane Nudge. Nudge.

Sarah There's tea made I'll get you some. I told your father not to get at you this morning, but he had a bad hangover. Still, at least he wasn't patronizing—or reasonable.

Jane He drinks too much.

Sarah At the moment—yes.

Jane And you take pills.

Sarah Yes.

Jane I don't know why you get so worked-up. There are worse things than moving house.

Sarah Yes, I know. Our worries don't register on the world problem-scale, but everything's relative.

Jane I've started writing a piece—for that magazine I told you about.

Sarah Oh yes. What on?

Jane Teenage abortion.

Sarah (*with distaste*) Is this going to be a personal reminiscence?

Jane Yes, but I'm going to do some research as well. I read that over one-hundred-and-fifty thousand women had abortions in Britain last year.

Sarah If you're going to talk to all of them, won't it take . . .

Jane Oh Mum! Don't start criticizing already. I'm not going to ask you to publish it.

Sarah Look, it is still possible to get a job *after* you've left college.

Jane Did you?

Sarah Yes. For a while.

Jane A very short while. And then you got married and had kids.

Sarah (*hurt*) You talk as if you aren't one of them.

Jane All right, but half the time you wished you were out of the house doing something else, didn't you? I don't want that to happen to me.

Sarah (*irritably*) We're not asking you to get married. We're suggesting you go back to college and . . .

Jane I've told you, Mum, I hate the course. That's why I'm glad all this happened.

Sarah If you only got yourself pregnant as a protest against English literature there must be easier ways. You could just change courses.

Jane And that solves everything!

Sarah Nothing solves everything. You're getting to sound like Ben. He's always looking for total solutions.

Jane At least he's had the guts to go his own way.

Sarah So are you going to follow his example? Drop out? Follow every crackpot trend, and end up talking pious jibberish into a tape-recorder?

Jane Look, at least he believes in what he does.

Sarah And we don't, is that it?

Phone rings

Our children have seen the light. Hallelujah!

She looks from Jane to the phone in equal disgust, and goes out

Jane (*answering the phone*) Hello. (*Her face falls*) Oh! Simon. Who told you I was here? . . . I'm fine. Look, I told you it won't work. I'm sorry, but . . . No, Simon, I'm not coming back . . . Yes, that's it. I'm . . . (*Angrily*) No, you listen . . . Don't you—

The door opens and Jimmy comes in whistling. He sees Jane on the phone

—don't you talk to me like that . . . (*She sees Jimmy, and has a brain-wave. She puts her hand over the mouthpiece*) Jimmy, could you deal with this? It's an obscene phone call.

Jimmy takes phone and listens with horror for a moment

Jimmy (*into the phone*) Yeah, well that's your problem, mate. (*He bangs the phone down*)

Black-out

Jimmy and Jane exit

During the following taped dialogue, Jane changes and then she and Liz enter and sit on the sofa

In the darkness there is the sound of scraping and hammering and then Jimmy whistling loud and clear

Frank's voice Oh hell, no. What's he doing here? It's Saturday.
Sarah's voice He's finishing off in Ben's room.
Frank's voice It sounds as if he's in bed with me.
Sarah's voice I'm going out. You sleep in.
Frank's voice Sleep—with that racket.
Sarah's voice If you've got a request, I'll ask him.

There is the sound of a door shutting

The Lights come up

Jane and Liz sit on the sofa drinking coffee. Jane looks slightly sprucer and more cheerful. Liz is dressed for going away

Liz How are you feeling now?
Jane Much better. I felt lousy before—really depressed.
Liz You're bound to. Everyone does.
Jane Have you ever had one?
Liz Yes. Once.
Jane Could we talk about it sometime?
Liz Yes, of course.
Jane I'm writing a piece about it—for a new women's magazine. Of course I can tell Mum finds the idea distasteful. She's so bloody conventional.

Sarah appears in the kitchen, hears them and stops to listen

Liz Sarah would call that having standards. They make her feel safe.
Jane But she imposes them on everyone else.
Liz Not if you don't let her. I didn't.
Jane She isn't your mother.
Liz She used to act as though she was.

Sarah comes in, trying not to look upset. Again she is interrupting a cosy scene from which she is being excluded in her own house. She carries a shopping basket

Sarah Good-morning.

Jane looks uncomfortable at the thought she might have been overheard. Liz remains relaxed

Liz Hello. Have you had breakfast?
Sarah It's half-past ten. What time are you leaving?
Liz Any minute. I promised Mum I'd be there for lunch.
Sarah I'm going to pop out and get some bread. I'll get a cake you can take her.
Liz That would be nice.

   Sarah goes out

Jane Do you think she heard us?
Liz Probably. Is that so terrible?
Jane I've said worse to her, but not to anyone else. (*After a pause*) I just wish we didn't fight all the time. She's been so busy trying to control our lives she's forgotten about hers.
Liz Maybe that's what she chose to do.
Jane Yes, but it must be frustrating—she's very bright really. She just needs to get out and do a decent job.
Liz Don't we all!
Jane Are you just going for the weekend?
Liz Yes. Then I'm going back to my place.
Jane Could I come with you?
Liz Why not?

Jimmy is heard whistling, off

Jane Oh God, the phantom whistler.

   Jimmy comes in, carrying a thick volume of "Decline and Fall of the Roman Empire"

Jimmy Morning.
Liz Morning.
Jane Hello.
Jimmy No rehearsals today?
Liz No.

He goes to put the book back in the bookcase

   Oh, still on *War and Peace*?
Jimmy No. *Decline and Fall of the Roman Empire*. Makes a change.
Jane (*to Liz*) I'll go and pack my bag.

   Jane exits cheerfully

Jimmy More cheerful today, isn't she?
Liz Yes.
Jimmy Got over her spot of bother, has she?
Liz That's right.
Jimmy Difficult age that. Especially for girls. I'm glad I've only got a son. They've got a son too, haven't they?

Liz Yes.

Jimmy In America?

Liz Yes. We've got an aunt in New Zealand too.

Jimmy Oh, I don't mean to sound nosey. Interested in people, that's all. You don't know how frustrating this job can be, if you are. You work on someone's house—you see and hear some strange bloody things though I can tell you. But then they go off and finish the scene in another room. You never discover how it works out. It's like having to leave before the end of a film.

Liz That's interesting. I've never thought of it that way before. (*She goes towards the kitchen with the tray of coffee things*)

The doorbell rings

Jimmy Shall I get it?

Liz Thanks.

Jimmy goes out to open the front door

Liz quickly takes the coffee things into the kitchen

John (*off*) Are Mr and Mrs Gladwin in, please?

Jimmy (*off*) Mrs Gladwin's out at the moment. Mr Gladwin's in the bathroom if you'd like to come in I'll tell Mr Gladwin you're here. What was the name again?

John and Beryl Fearnley come into the living-room, followed by Jimmy

John Fearnley. You're—er—working here?

Jimmy Yes. That's right.

John Does that mean the Gladwins aren't moving then?

Jimmy Oh no, they're still moving, but they've had a bit of a problem here. You see—they've had some sub—

Liz comes out of the kitchen very fast

John What sort of problem?

Liz Hello.

Beryl recognizes Liz as "Mrs Smith" from her last visit. She is clearly upset at this

Baryl Oh Mrs Smith, isn't it?

Liz That's right. You're Mrs—

Beryl Mrs Fearnley.

Liz You were here before when I was looking round.

Beryl Yes. Is your husband with you this time?

Liz No. He's not back from Geneva yet.

John Then the house is still for sale.

Liz Oh yes. This gentleman—kindly let me in—you see—Mrs Gladwin is out.

John (*to Jimmy*) You said there was a problem with the house, what is it?

Jimmy Ahh—well—last week they . . .

Liz (*heavily to Jimmy*) The Fearnleys have come to look at the house too.

John What is the problem?

Jimmy Aah. Well . . . Nothing much really. Little leak from a bathroom pipe. Just been fixing it up. They were very lucky. Didn't do much damage to speak of. I mean, I said to them if you're moving why don't you leave it to the new people to fix it up, save yourself the expense, but they said *no*—it was *their* responsibility. Very nice people, the Gladwins, they . . .

Liz Go and tell Mr Gladwin that there's more people here.

Jimmy Oh. Yes. Right.

Jimmy goes out

Liz and the Fearnleys eye each other awkwardly. As before, Liz has manoeuvred herself into a position where she has little alternative but to leave the house

Liz Well, I'd better be going. Lovely room, isn't it?

John Yes.

Beryl Very nice.

Liz They don't build houses like this anymore.

There is the sound of the front door opening and shutting

Sarah comes in with her shopping basket, with a cake-box on top of the bread. She takes in the situation as best she can

Sarah Oh! Hello.

Beryl Hello, Mrs Gladwin. We are sorry to barge in on you like this, but we were passing, and I was so upset when I heard.

John Perhaps we ought to let Mrs Smith finish looking round first.

Sarah Mrs Smith? (*Looking at Liz, the penny dropping*) Oh yes. You're here again?

Liz Oh, I've finished, Mrs Gladwin. That nice *plumber* of yours let me in. He explained to me about the leak. Lucky it did so little damage.

Jane comes in. She carries her duffel-bag, looks cheerful, and is reasonably spruced-up. Her eye falls on Liz before she notices the Fearnleys

Jane I'm ready when you are, Liz.

Liz Ah, Jane. You haven't met Mrs Gladwin yet, have you? It's her house. This is my daughter.

Sarah How do you do?

Jane hasn't got the faintest idea what's going on. Both she and Sarah look stunned and shake hands

Liz (*to Jane*) There was no need to bring your bag in here, dear. You could have left it in the car.

Frank comes into, for him, an incomprehensible scene

I've just collected her from the airport. She's at finishing school—in Switzerland. Ah, you must be Mr Gladwin. Very nice to meet you.

Frank, mystified, acknowledges this fact. They shake hands

Sarah This is Mrs Smith and *her* daughter.

Frank Oh, morning.

Liz Yes, well, we'd better be going. My daughter and I are going to see my mother now.

Sarah Mother?

Liz Don't want to be late.

Beryl Is your mother any better?

Liz Better? Oh yes, much better now, thanks.

Beryl Can she recognize you now?

There is a silence while the penny doesn't drop for Liz, who hasn't got a good memory of her own lines. She suddenly remembers

Liz Oh, yes. It turned out to be—chicken-pox. Goodbye, everybody.

Liz steers Jane out

Frank clearly doesn't understand any of this. Sarah realizes she has still got the cake-box for Liz. She takes the box out of her basket, and is about to call after her, but she realizes there is no way to explain giving her a cake in front of the Fearnleys. She puts it back in the basket

John We're a . . .

Beryl We're sorry to barge in on you like this. But we were passing, and we saw the "For Sale" sign still up, and I said to my husband, because I'd been so upset when I heard . . .

John My wife called your estate-agent on Wednesday and spoke to someone there who said the house had been taken off the market . . . I don't really trust these estate-agents not to play games with everybody.

Beryl I knew you were moving and it seemed very odd, I wanted to get back to you last week because our friends in Skegness got in touch with us on Tuesday. They've as good as sold their house to some people from Goole, and so on Wednesday . . .

John We just thought we'd make sure ourselves whether your house was still for sale. Of course, if you've sold it to somebody else . . .

Beryl If that Mrs Smith has made an offer . . .

Sarah Mrs Smith? Oh no. She keeps dropping in.

Frank doesn't understand any of this

Beryl Oh good. I was so upset. The whole week . . .

John So the agent misled us.

Frank Oh they always get things wrong.

There is silence. Beryl gives John a heavy hint by looking at him

John Well, what I'd like to do is offer you your asking-price now. My solicitor will get in touch with yours on Monday. But I want to shake hands on it now. I don't want anybody else coming along . . .

Sarah sticks her hand out instantly

Frank Hold on. We have to complete on our flat in four weeks. You'd have to exchange contracts by then.

John We'll try.

Beryl Oh, we would. I'm sure we could.

Frank And you'd have to complete four weeks after that. If *that's* an understanding I'll shake hands.

John Subject to survey, of course.

Frank Well, I suppose one can shake hands subject to survey.

Rather self-consciously he shakes hands with John. It is rather like a brief wedding-ceremony, with Sarah and Beryl as emotional witnesses

I must give you the name and address of my solicitor.

He and John go over to the desk, where Frank writes out the name and address of his solicitor. Beryl is near tears, she puts a hand on Sarah's arm

Beryl I'm so glad, so glad. It's been such a terrible week. I was so disappointed when the estate-agent said . . .

Sarah That was such a stupid mistake. I was furious.

Beryl I know we'll enjoy living here.

Sarah I'm sure you will.

Frank I'll let the agent know, and see he doesn't send anyone else.

John I'll get my solicitor on to this straight away. (*He takes the piece of paper from Frank*)

Beryl It's a lovely house. We'll take good care of it.

Sarah I know you will.

John (*going and taking Beryl's arm*) Well, we must let you get on with your day.

Beryl Thank you. Thank you so much.

John Goodbye.

Frank Do get in touch if there's anything you want.

John And I'll get on to my solicitor on Monday morning without fail.

John and Beryl go out and Frank accompanies them

Sarah is left close to tears

Frank comes back into the room

Frank I think we've really sold it this time.

Sarah Yes. I really think we have.

They hug each other

Thank God.

Black-out. The "Gloria" from Bach's "Magnificat in D" comes up full volume

Sarah exits and, when ready, Len, one of the removal men enters

As the "Gloria" ends the Lights come up on an almost bare room

Frank stands by the desk. He is on the phone. Len is rolling up the last carpet on the floor

Frank . . . I don't care if they're on the way to their solicitor. Look,

Laurence, I want to know the Fearnleys have signed the contract before you part with the completion money for the flat. I'm not moving out of here till they've signed.

Len reacts to this as he is taking out the carpet

I know they've accepted the survey, but there are other ways they can try to get the price down at the last minute . . .

Sarah (*off*) Oh, damn!

Bill (*off*) I'm sorry about that.

Sarah (*off*) Don't worry. That was my fault.

Frank (*on the phone*) . . . I've every right to be paranoid. Call me as soon as you know. I'm not moving otherwise. (*He slams the phone down*)

Sarah comes in, carrying "Jaws", which has been snapped in half

Sarah Broken "Jaws".

Frank Oh, no!

Sarah It's your fault. You just shoved them on top of a crate. (*She puts "Jaws" down on the desk*) What did Laurence say?

Frank Episode a hundred and nine. He's heard from the Fearnleys' solicitor. They are still on their way into his office to sign.

Sarah Why couldn't they have done it yesterday?

Frank The papers weren't in order. Bloody solicitors.

Sarah Why's it taking the Fearnleys so long to get in there?

Frank How do I know? Maybe they went in on her bicycle. I'm not moving till I know they've signed the contract on this house.

Sarah Nearly everything's in the van. They'll mutiny if you ask them to unload it.

Len and Bill come in

Bill All right if we take the desk now?

Sarah Yes.

Len and Bill go to take the desk. Frank picks up "Jaws"

Len What are they for?

Frank Very tough meat.

Sarah picks up the phone, while Len and Bill start to move the desk

Bill Got it, Len?

Len Yeah. Right.

They take the desk towards door

Bill Van's nearly loaded.

Sarah Good.

Frank Don't close the doors.

Len You are moving, aren't you?

Frank Not if—

Sarah Yes, of course we're moving.

Len and Bill go out with the desk

Sarah sadly watches her desk go. The phone in her hand rings. It startles her, but she doesn't answer it. Frank takes it from her

Frank Hello. Yes . . . Oh, thank God for that. They've actually done it? . . .

Sarah is watching him apprehensively. Frank gives her the thumbs up sign. Instead of relief, Sarah actually looks more worried. She goes over to the crate by the bookshelves, and takes out the copy of "War and Peace" that is on the top. She puts the book on the floor, and lies down in the Alexander Method

Yes, we'll only need the bridging-loan for a month. We'll survive . . . Yes, everything is almost packed. You must come and see the new place—when we get over this—in about five years I should think . . . Thanks, Laurence, bye. (*He turns and registers Sarah on the floor*) Sarah! What's wrong? Why are you lying there?

Sarah I'm talking to my muscles.

Frank Don't be daft, love. I haven't the strength to carry you out.

Sarah I feel terrible.

Frank What about?

Sarah Everything. It's as if *we're* being packed-up. Fourteen years of our lives put in a van. The children have left. Everything's suddenly gone.

Frank Come on. Ben will be back. Jane will soon get fed-up staying with Liz.

Sarah Oh God, they were right.

Frank Who were?

Sarah Liz and Jane.

Frank What about?

Sarah Me. I always wanted to be in control. Even when I wasn't I pretended I was. I can't pretend anymore.

Frank Nonsense. You've coped marvellously.

Sarah Coped! I hate that word. I can't face that flat.

Frank Sarah, we've just paid for it. Come on, you wanted a smaller place. You wanted a job.

Sarah That was ages ago. Now I just feel I need a pension.

Frank We're going to be all right. It'll be a bit like starting again.

Sarah I don't want to start again.

Len comes in with some letters

Len (*handing the letters to Frank*) The post's just been. (*He takes in Sarah*) Is she all right?

Sarah (*sitting up*) Yes. I'm all right.

Len picks up the last crate

Frank One for you from the office. God, the bills never stop.

Sarah takes the letter, sitting on the floor. She opens it and starts to read

Len This is the last crate.

Frank Good.

Len Just the garden stuff left.

Frank Right.

Len goes out with the crate

Sarah Oh dear!

Frank Is it about the job?

Sarah No. You never did ask your secretary about those pages, did you?

Frank Pages? What pages?

Sarah That manuscript.

Frank I forgot.

Sarah They've forwarded me a letter from the author. (*Reading*) "Dear Sirs, I sent you my novel *Away Game* in the strictest confidence. I cannot understand therefore why I have just had the first five pages returned to me from the *British Dental Journal* with a rejection-slip reading 'We are not in the habit of publishing fiction, let alone pornography. However, we find your article *Recent Research into Plaque Control* most interesting. Are you a dentist? If you could provide us with some background information on yourself—we would be happy to publish it.' "

Frank (*looking at his envelopes*) Oh hell! I didn't tell the electricity and the gas company we were moving.

Sarah No. You told me to. Remember?

Frank Did you?

Sarah Yes. They came earlier and read the meters.

Frank What would I do without you?

He helps her up from the floor

Sarah Pay two lots of gas and electricity bills—and listen to Vivaldi in peace.

Bill comes in

Bill We're just about ready to move off.

Frank All right. We'll see you there.

Bill goes out

That's it then.

They both look round the bare room

Sarah Completion! It's as awful as it sounds.

Frank Well, a deep breath and let's go. Don't forget your book. You may want to lie down at the new place.

Sarah (*picking up her book, noticing the "SOLD" sign*) Look. They've put up the "Sold" sign already.

He goes and looks, putting his arm around her

Frank Don't waste any time, do they?

Sarah We suffer and they get all the publicity.

They go towards the door and the phone rings. As usual, Sarah registers it, but doesn't answer it. Frank looks at it and ignores it too

He takes Sarah's arm and they go out, leaving the phone ringing

CURTAIN

FURNITURE AND PROPERTY LIST

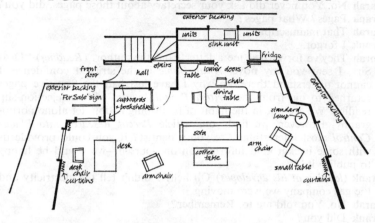

ACT I

On stage: Sofa. *On it:* cushions

2 armchairs. *On them:* cushions

Coffee-table. *On it:* magazines, cigarette lighter, ashtray

2 small occasional tables

Desk. *On it:* manuscripts, desk lamp, cassette tape, phone, viewing list, notepad, pens etc. *In drawer:* bottle of tablets, pocket calculator, manuscript

Desk chair

Carpets

Window curtains—open to start

Cupboards UR with shelves above. *On shelves:* hardbound and paperback books, including large, hardbound volume of *War and Peace*, table lamp

Cupboards along R wall. *In upper one:* bottles of liqueurs, including one of Green Chartreuse, wine glasses, liqueur glasses, sherry glasses. *In lower one:* rack of records including Vivaldi's *Concerto for Three Violins and Orchestra in F Major* and Vivaldi's *Concerto for Guitar and Strings in D Major*, half-empty sherry bottle. *On lower cupboard top:* hi-fi system, tray containing sherry decanter, bottle of whisky, and assortment of glasses and soda siphon

Bookshelves under U bay window. *On them:* manuscripts, box-files books

Folding dining-table

4 dining-chairs

Fireplace. *Above it:* mirror
Standard lamp
Outside u *bay window:* "FOR SALE" notice

IN KITCHEN
Extractor fan set in window
Sink unit
Kitchen units
Fridge. *In it:* milk
Kettle
Teapot

Personal: **Sarah:** wristwatch, reading glasses (used throughout play)
            Frank: wristwatch
            Peter: compass
            John: pen, retractable steel tape-measure

During 1st Black-out

Strike: Used sherry and whisky glass

        IN KITCHEN

Set: 2 glasses

During 2nd Black-out

Set: Window curtains open
      On dining-table: tape-recorder with "Ben" tape, copy of *The Guardian*,
          tray containing rack of toast, packet of cornflakes, coffee-pot,
          cutlery and crockery for 2
      On coffee-table: pile of official-looking documents, several folders,
          mounted model of a set of jaws

Off stage: Briefcase **(Frank)**

During 3rd Black-out

Set: *On dining-table:* 2 place settings, 2 plates of tuna fish salad, plate of
      rolls, 2 glass water tumblers

        IN KITCHEN

      Corkscrew
      Cheese board with cheese
      Tray
      Pair of dark glasses and long, silk scarf (for **Liz**)

Off stage: Holdall containing two bottles of white wine with plastic lids, short,
         fur jacket, handbag containing cigarettes **(Liz)**

During 4th Black-out

Set: IN KITCHEN
      Chopping knife

Off stage: Briefcase **(Frank)**
         Shopping **(Liz)**

During 5th Black-out

Personal: **Sarah:** cup of coffee
     Joan: retractable steel tape-measure

     IN KITCHEN
     Cup of coffee (for **Liz**)

During 6th Black-out

Personal: **Frank:** *Journal of Periodontology*
     Peter: notebook

Off stage: Full shopping basket, plastic carrier bag **(Sarah)**

ACT II

Strike: Scattered manuscript
Set: Living-room door wedged open
     Dust sheet covering floor-area around door
     Step-ladder open by door lintel. *By it:* paint-pot containing brushes
       and mixing-stick, pot of paint and brush
     Plaster cracks above door filled in
     IN KITCHEN
     Mug of tea **(Sarah)**
     Cup of tea **(Liz)**
     Tray. *On it:* two mugs of tea and sugar bowl **(Jimmy)**
Off stage: Script **(Liz)**
     Duffel-bag **(Jane)**

During 1st Black-out

Strike: Dust sheet
Set: New squares of colour above lintel to contrast slightly with old
Off stage: Evening paper **(Frank)**

During 2nd Black-out

Set: Window curtains closed
     On sofa: notepad, pen and manuscript (for **Sarah**)
     On dining-table: salad and portion of quiche on plate
     IN KITCHEN
     Wine-glass
     In fridge: half-full bottle of white wine

During 3rd Black-out
Set: IN KITCHEN
     Glass of water with spoon
     Tin of bicarb

During 4th Black-out

Strike: *From coffee-table:* bottle of Green Chartreuse, glass, spoon, 2 sherry
     glasses

Set: *On dining-table:* jug of milk, packet of cornflakes, rack of toast,
            coffee-pot, cutlery and crockery for 4, folded copy of *The Guardian*
            Window curtains open
            In armchair: **Frank's** jacket and briefcase

            IN KITCHEN
            Mug of tea **(Jimmy)**

Off stage: Letters including 1 airmail **(Liz)**

During 5th Black-out

Strike: *From dining-table:* packet of cornflakes, jug of milk, any cutlery or
            crockery remaining, letters and copy of *The Guardian*
Set: *On coffee-table:* tray containing 2 coffee-cups and saucers, coffee-pot

            IN KITCHEN
            Empty shopping basket

Off stage: Volume of *Decline And Fall Of The Roman Empire* **(Jimmy)**
            Loaf of bread, cake-box **(Sarah)**
            Duffel-bag **(Jane)**

During 6th Black-out

Strike: Sofa
            2 armchairs
            Coffee-table
            2 small occasional tables
            Standard lamp
            Desk chair
            All carpets except for 1 almost rolled up
            Dining-table and chairs
            Mirror
            From bookshelves under window: manuscripts, box-files, books
            From lower cupboard top: hi-fi unit, drinks' tray and glasses
            From shelves UR: lamp
            From desk top: manuscripts, desk lamp, portable typewriter, cassette
            tape, tape-recorder, notepad, pens etc, **Sarah's** handbag

            IN KITCHEN
            Kettle
            Teapot
            Any dressing on units

Set: "SOLD" sign on "FOR SALE" notice

Re-set: Books from UR shelves in crate with copy of *War And Peace* on top

Off stage: Broken model of set of jaws **(Sarah)**
            Letters **(Len)**

LIGHTING PLOT

Practical fittings required: 2 wall-bracket lights either side of mirror, standard lamp, table lamp, desk lamp, pendant light in kitchen

Interior. A living-room, kitchen and hall. The same scene throughout

ACT I

To open: Black-out

Cue 1	Doorbell rings *Bring up hall lighting, standard lamp and* UR *lamp with covering spots, and exterior lighting with sunset effect through* L *window. As exterior gradually fades increase interior*	(Page 2)
Cue 2	**Sarah** switches on kitchen light *Snap on kitchen pendant and covering spots*	(Page 6)
Cue 3	**Sarah** switches off kitchen light *Snap off kitchen pendant and covering spots*	(Page 6)
Cue 4	**Sarah** switches off standard lamp *Snap off standard lamp and covering spots*	(Page 10)
Cue 5	**Sarah** switches off wall-bracket lights *Snap off wall-bracket lights and covering spots*	(Page 10)
Cue 6	**Frank** switches off UR lamp *Snap off* UR *lamp and covering spots*	(Page 10)
Cue 7	**Frank** closes door *Black-out*	(Page 10)
Cue 8	Sound of door opening and closing quietly off *Bring up exterior moonlight effect*	(Page 10)
Cue 9	**Frank** switches on UR lamp *Snap on* UR *lamp and covering spots*	(Page 10)
Cue 10	**Frank** opens fridge door *Snap on fridge lighting and then off as door closes*	(Page 11)
Cue 11	**Frank** switches on desk lamp *Snap on desk lamp and covering spots*	(Page 11)
Cue 12	**Sarah** opens fridge door *Snap on fridge lighting*	(Page 13)
Cue 13	**Frank** turns off desk lamp *Snap off desk lamp and covering spots*	(Page 13)
Cue 14	**Sarah** closes fridge door *Snap off fridge lighting*	(Page 13)
Cue 15	**Frank** switches off UR lamp *Snap of* UR *lamp and covering spots*	(Page 14)

Cue 16	**Sarah** and **Frank** exit *Black-out*	(Page 14)
Cue 17	**Ben's voice:** ". . . four evenings a week." *Bring up overall summer morning effect*	(Page 14)
Cue 18	**Sarah:** ". . . four inch dwarf." *Black-out*	(Page 17)
Cue 19	**Sarah's voice:** ". . . unfair to the author." *Bring up bright midday effect with sunshine through* R *window*	(Page 18)
Cue 20	**Sarah** drifts off to sleep *Fade to Black-out, pause, then bring up early evening light* *with sunset through* L *window*	(Page 27)
Cue 21	**Frank:** "We're selling to the Bellings." *Fade to Black-out. When ready bring up overall bright* *daylight with sun through* R *window*	(Page 30)
Cue 22	**Sarah:** ". . . my curtains, carpets and kitchen." *Slow fade to Black-out*	(Page 32)
Cue 23	**Laurence's voice:** ". . . and here." (fourth time) *Bring up overall bright daylight with sun through* R *window*	(Page 33)

ACT II

To open: Black-out

Cue 24	*Getting To Know You* being whistled *Bring up overall bright daylight effect*	(Page 36)
Cue 25	**Jimmy** exits *Black-out. When ready bring up early evening effect with* *sunset through* L *window*	(Page 42)
Cue 26	**Frank** goes out *Black-out*	(Page 44)
Cue 27	As music and knocking die down *Bring up standard lamp, wall-bracket lights,* UR *lamp and* *covering spots with night exterior*	(Page 44)
Cue 28	**Jane** opens fridge door *Snap on fridge lighting and then off as door closes*	(Page 44)
Cue 29	**Sarah** turns off standard lamp *Snap off standard lamp and covering spots*	(Page 46)
Cue 30	**Sarah** switches off wall-bracket lights *Snap off wall-bracket lights and covering spots*	(Page 46)
Cue 31	**Sarah** switches off UR lamp *Black-out, short pause, then bring up hall lighting and night* *exterior*	(Page 46)
Cue 32	**Frank** switches on UR lamp *Snap on* UR *lamp and covering spots*	(Page 47)
Cue 33	**Frank** switches on standard lamp *Snap on standard lamp and covering spots*	(Page 47)
Cue 34	**Sarah** switches on kitchen light *Snap on kitchen pendant with covering spots*	(Page 49)

Cue 35 **Sarah** switches off kitchen light   (Page 49)
        Snap off kitchen pendant and covering spots

Cue 36 **Frank** storms out, banging the door   (Page 51)
        Black-out

Cue 37 The banging becomes intermittent   (Page 51)
        Bring up overall summer morning light

Cue 38 **Jimmy** bangs the phone down   (Page 57)
        Black-out

Cue 39 There is the sound of a door shutting   (Page 57)
        Bring up overall summer morning light

Cue 40 **Sarah:** "Thank God."   (Page 62)
        Black-out

Cue 41 As the "Gloria" ends   (Page 62)
        Bring up overall bright daylight with sun through R *window*

EFFECTS PLOT

ACT I

| Cue 19 | **Sarah** switches off kettle
Fade kettle whistle | (Page 34) |

ACT II

Cue 20	When the CURTAIN rises *Effect of builder's general bustle: hammering, bricks being broken and chipped, ladders and furniture being moved, with* **Jimmy** *whistling "Hello, Young Lovers" slightly out of tune*	(Page 36)
Cue 21	As the Lights come up on **Jimmy** painting *Banging from the back of the house*	(Page 36)
Cue 22	**Jimmy**: ". . . I'm to do a proper job . . ." *Phone rings*	(Page 36)
Cue 23	**Jimmy** shrugs *Phone rings*	(Page 39)
Cue 24	**Jane**: ". . . for twenty-four hours." *Kettle whistles, quickly turned off*	(Page 40)
Cue 25	**Sarah**: "Yes. Of course." *Phone rings*	(Page 41)
Cue 26	Black-out *Tape of* **Jimmy** *whistling loudly*	(Page 42)
*Cue 27	Black-out *"Jericho" plays with tape of* **Frank's voice** *and knocking on door. Sounds reach a crescendo and then fade*	(Page 44)
*Cue 28	**Jane** switches on tape-recorder *Tape of* **Sarah's voice**	(Page 45)
Cue 29	**Frank** switches on hi-fi and then turns down volume *Vivaldi's "Concerto for Guitar and Strings in D Major" plays loudly and then turned down*	(Page 47)
Cue 30	**Frank** switches off hi-fi *Snap off music*	(Page 47)
*Cue 31	Black-out *Tape of hammering, knocking on a door,* **Sarah's** *and* **Frank's voices** *with the banging and hammering continuing intermittently until a few moments after the Lights come up*	(Page 51)
Cue 32	**Liz**: ". . . to sell half a house?" *Sound of letters falling through letter-box*	(Page 52)
Cue 33	**Jimmy** goes to the sink *Sound of running tap*	(Page 53)
Cue 34	**Liz**: "O.K." *Kettle whistles*	(Page 54)
Cue 35	**Liz** switches off kettle *Fade kettle whistle*	(Page 54)
Cue 36	**Sarah**: ". . . is that it?" *Phone rings*	(Page 56)

Cues marked with an asterisk indicate the effect contains pre-recorded sections
of the dialogue

MADE AND PRINTED IN GREAT BRITAIN BY
LATIMER TREND & COMPANY LTD PLYMOUTH
MADE IN ENGLAND

*Cue 37 Black-out   (Page 57)
Tape of scraping and hammering, Jimmy shouting, Frank's and Sarah's voices and door shutting

Cue 38 Liz goes towards the kitchen   (Page 59)
Doorbell rings

Cue 39 Black-out   (Page 62)
"Clonn" from Bach's "Menuhin in D" comes up full volume

Cue 40 As Liz and Bill go out with the desk   (Page 64)
Phone rings

Cue 41 Sarah and Frank go towards the door   (Page 65)
Phone rings

Cues marked with an asterisk indicate the effect contains pre-recorded sections of the dialogue.

MADE AND PRINTED IN GREAT BRITAIN BY
LATIMER TREND & COMPANY LTD PLYMOUTH
MADE IN ENGLAND